A COURSE

OF

CLINICAL LECTURES

ON DIPHTHERIA.

DELIVERED BEFORE THE CLASS OF

HAHNEMANN MEDICAL COLLEGE, CHICAGO,

SESSION OF 1862-3.

BY R. LUDLAM, M. D.,

PROFESSOR OF PHYSIOLOGY, PATHOLOGY, AND CLINICAL MEDICINE.

CHICAGO:
C. S. HALSEY, 136 CLARK STREET.

1863.

DUNLOP, SEWELL & SPALDING,
PRINTERS.
40 Clark St., Chicago.

TO

The Alumni

OF

THE HAHNEMANN MEDICAL COLLEGE

THESE LECTURES

ARE RESPECTFULLY DEDICATED

BY THEIR FRIEND AND

FELLOW-STUDENT

THE AUTHOR

PREFACE.

In the preparation of the Clinical Lectures on Diphtheria, the design was to afford a practical digest of the disease and its treatment. The kind and appreciative spirit in which the fruits of this labor were received by the Class, to whom they were first delivered, suggested the possibility that, in a published form, they might prove equally acceptable to the general profession. Hence another work upon Diphtheria.

With an expression of personal obligation to those who have already accomplished so much in the same direction, the Author is led to hope that this contribution to the literature of the subject may be of essential service to his brethren in the profession.

CHICAGO, 87 CLARK ST., March, 1863.

INDEX.

CLINICAL LECTURES

ON DIPHTHERIA.

LECTURE I.

DEFINITION OF.—VARIETIES.—*Two forms of.—Incorrect nomenclature.—Both forms essentially one.—Not a new disease.—Cause of difference in types.—These convertible.—* DIPHTHERIA SIMPLEX.—*Case.—Analysis of Symptoms.—The Fever.—The Tongue and Digestive Symptoms.—The Throat.—The Odor of the Breath.—Case.—The Coryza.—The Cough.—The Gastric Symptoms.—The Eruption.—The Disorders of the Urinary Function.—The Local and General Debility.*

GENTLEMEN :—

DIPHTHERIA, or Diphthérite, is a word used to signify a specific constitutional affection, which should be classed among the zymoses, and is characterized, locally, by the formation of a false membrane upon mucous or abraded cutaneous surfaces.

VARIETIES.—Practically speaking, I am of opinion that we should recognize but *two* forms of this disease, viz: the simple and the malignant—Diphtheria Simplex and Diphtheria Maligna. I am aware that other classifications have been recommended by eminent professional authorities, but prefer this as more simple and available than either. The phrase,

2

"Croupal Diphtheria," as proposed by the Lancet Sanitary Commission, for a third variety of the affection, signifies nothing more than a complication of the two diseases, croup and diphtheria. It would be equally proper to apply the adjectives scarlatinal, typhus, typhoid, erysipelatous, ophthalmic, abdominal or uterine, to the various modifications due to specific functional and structural lesions, incident to this disease. It would be improper to speak of cardiac diphtheria, and yet, pathologically considered, we must regard this phrase as equally correct as the "croupal" diphtheria offered by the aforesaid Commission.

Let us be plain and explicit. The best possible results in their treatment will spring of this distinction between the diphtheria simplex and the diphtheria maligna. That in nature they are essentially the same, there is but little doubt. In this they resemble the two forms of cholera, the cholera morbus and the cholera maligna. The points of resemblance are found to extend to the manner and time of their prevalence. These two general varieties of disease have, indeed, no very intimate relation. But we call your attention to a fact hitherto overlooked by the profession—that, as the Asiatic cholera prevails every year in the modified form of an endemic—the cholera morbus; so the diptheria maligna—an epidemic whose terrible ravages are not less to be dreaded, has become more familiar and less fearful in the guise of an endemic, the diphtheria simplex.

You will not understand me as implying that the diphtheria is a new disease, one with which the earlier physicians were not more or less familiar. Its medical history has been traced back to a period almost as ancient as that of Homer. I believe the milder form of the disease is endemic to this part of North America. The better class of pathologists among us have always recognized sporadic ceses of throat affection, with certain symptoms and sequelæ, which prevented their being classified among the different forms, either of angina, croup, or scarlatina.

The two types of diphtheria differ in proportion as they

are modified by season, climate, epidemic constitution of the atmosphere, and other sources of propagation and development of a specific zymotic cause, as well as in the individual organic susceptibilities of persons who are seized.

These contingencies make the types convertible. In a single house, or upon one street, every case may prove to be mild and tractable. Next door, or around the corner, the very converse of this is true. Here, almost every attack proves fatal. In rural districts, one practitioner may find little difficulty in bringing all his cases to a successful termination; while his neighbor, the limits of whose circuit lie near his own, and who is equally skillful, is just as unsuccessful. Or in a family of children, one may have the disease in the more severe, and the others in the milder form. In this regard, as well as in the fact that children seized with the diphtheria at a later period of its prevalence do not have it so badly as at first, it resembles scarlatina and other epidemic disorders.

DIPHTHERIA SIMPLEX.

Case.—Eva R., a little girl of four years, is usually well and healthy; not predisposed to croup or any throat affection. Has been ill four days. The early symptoms were a general malaise, with a mild degree of fever, a pungent heat of the skin, neither preceded by chill nor followed by perspiration. The first paroxysm continued through the night, but subsided in the morning into a marked remission. Pulse 100. The tongue became slightly furred, and a little red at the tip and edges. The fauces, uvula and tonsils appeared a little swollen and injected. The mucous membrane covering these parts is of a light mahogany hue. The tonsils are somewhat swollen externally, and but slightly sensitive to pressure. The breath is very offensive, having the peculiar diphtheritic odor. There are no false membranes visible in the superior air passages. She makes but little complaint in swallowing either food or drinks. Has a troublesome coryza, the discharge from the nasal outlet being somewhat acrid and corrosive. The cough is occasional, with a loud, but not shrill sound. It is dry and unsatisfactory, and renewed in slight paroxysms, as in acute influenza, affecting the bronchial mucous membrane. The voice becomes a little hoarse, especially towards evening. The only pain experienced is referred to the epigastrium. This was of a cutting, colicky nature, and would intermit for half or three-fourths of an hour, and then return, lasting only a few minutes. As the paroxysm would begin to subside, she complained of slight nausea, but has vomited in all only twice. The abdominal parietes are not tympanitic, neither flaccid, relaxed, nor yet too hot to the touch. She has had no diarrhœa. The urine is scanty, muddy, and voided at long intervals. The eruption is slight, and resembles that of rubeola. It made its first appearance last evening. These symptoms have continued with but slight modification, to the present time; the fever has developed into a remittent type, the exacerbation occurring reguarly every evening, the paroxysm lasting until two in the morning, and going off without diaphoresis. While the fever is upon her, she is flighty and temporarily delirious. If she sleep for a few moments, she is sure to awaken with symptoms of fright, not recognizing her mother or those about her. In a very little while she becomes rational, but remains nervous and irritable. The pupil is seen to contract and dilate—now, it is of the natural size, and again, without any apparent cause, it may be while she is looking at you, it becomes dilated to almost the whole extent of the iris. In a twinkling, it is contracted again. The pulse, at present, is 120, the heart-sounds are quite normal, and the vesicular resonance well marked over the entire chest. She is cheerful, and even playful—thinks she should not be confined in her room, or even within doors.

Here, gentlemen, is a case of Diphtheria Simplex. Let us analyze the symptoms presented:

The Fever.—So far as my individual observation extends, this form of the diphtheria is more uniformly ushered in, and accompanied throughout its course by febrile symptoms, than is the diphtheria maligna. The height of the fever, however, does not appear proportional to the severity of the attack. Some of the mildest examples of this disease are characterized by the most violent febrile paroxysms, while the opposite is true of those cases which, from the outset, are more decidedly virulent in their nature. Its type is nearly always remittent, although it may sometimes, and in certain localities will become either continued, or indeed intermittent. The paroxysm usually recurs at evening, and is marked by a hot, dry skin, with burning of the hands and feet for the relief of which the little patient, if old enough, desires to be sponged off with warm water. In some cases, there is a paroxysmal headache, which comes on each evening with the febrile stage, and declines along with it. This headache is generally accompanied by a lameness and stiffness in the muscular cords on one side or another of the neck. The heat of skin is very marked, and pungent enough almost to burn when one touches it. It resembles the contact with a hot iron or stove, and gives one the sensation as if it would "*siss*," should we apply the washerwoman's test to the surface. After some hours, this symptom is almost entirely wanting. The general heat of the skin has declined, but there is no moisture to follow in its train, or minister to its relief. When the febrile paroxysm has passed away, the cutaneous integment has cooled off, and no excess of temperature is observable anywhere upon the surface of the body, save around the neck, and in the axillæ and the groins. When the type of the fever is continuous, this symptom persists for a longer period. In either case, however, it appears characteristic that its decline is almost never accompanied by a free flow of the sensible perspiration, neither by a copious diuresis. We shall draw a therapeutical hint from this fact a little farther on.

In a majority of cases, the pulse is much the same as in the ordinary infantile remittent fever. During the febrile exacerbation, it will, as a matter of course, be considerably accelerated, its regularity, frequency, etc., being modified by contingencies of age, sex, type of the disease, and temperament. In the diphtheria simplex, for a child of six years, it rarely exceeds 115 to 120 during the height of the fever.

The Tongue, and Digestive Symptoms.—The tongue presents different appearances, in proportion as the throat symptoms are more or less violent, and as the alimentary sympathies are disturbed in a greater or less degree. If the throat is more decidedly affected, the tongue will be coated with a dirty, yellowish-white fur; or it may be covered with a thin, whitish coating, which shall have a ragged, serrated appearance, as if by accident the teeth had torn away a portion thereof, and left the surface of the organ beneath almost entirely denuded and raw, like a piece of beef. Gastric complication would be indicated by a fiery red tongue, the unnatural color being either diffuse, or limited to its tip and margins. If the intestinal mucous surfaces are decidedly affected, we may look for a dark, brownish tint of its exterior, with more or less of sordes upon the teeth, and general adynamia. In some examples of diphtheria simplex, these latter symptoms are present from the outset; again, they advance insidiously, and appear only at a later period of the disease. Not unfrequently the tongue has an apthous appearance, its edges and tip being studded with occasional small ulcers. I have known such symptoms to be diagnosed and treated as "canker rash," or ulcerative stomatitis. In some cases, the patient complains of sharp, smarting, biting pains in these diseased spots; while in others, the same suffering is experienced in the whole oral mucous membrane. The mouth feels as if it had been cauterized by one of the mineral acids.

The Throat.—Many physicians insist that the presence of a patch of false membrane upon the tonsils or fauces is a pathognomonic and ever-present symptom of genuine diphtheria. If, in a given case, all the remaining signs, local and general, of this disorder were present, and this one still wanting, they would decide the case was not one of diphtheria. Modern pathology discards this view of its significance. Multiplied observation and research establish that the deposit may occur upon any portion of the free surface of either the mucous membranes, or of denuded cutaneous integument upon the exterior of the body. The exudation is simply the local result of the general disease, and may or may not be wanting. In a few cases the complaint runs its entire course without any visible deposit about the throat or upon the tonsils. Now and then a patient dies suddenly, without having suffered any inconvenience whatever from swelling or inflammation in this vicinity, and morbid deposits may be altogether wanting.

In diphtheria simplex, we rarely find the throat and fauces very considerably inflamed. There is usually some tumefaction which may be limited in extent to the uvula, to one or both the tonsils, the velum palati, the respiratory compartment of the pharynx, or may involve them all. The mucous membrane covering the affected parts appears congested, and of a dusky red, mottled, or of a light mahogany color. Sometimes it is of a pinkish hue. The patient complains of slight prickling pains, with soreness in the fauces, which by-and-by extends along the Eustachian tube into the ear. The difficulty in swallowing will be proportioned to the severity of the local inflammation, which may dip down into the subjacent integument, and so invole the more contractile parts; and also to the tumefaction of the tonsil glands, which, from their increased size, may interfere with the passage of the ingesta. Difficult deglutition is not, however, common to this form of the affection, unless it be in those cases which degenerate into the more malignant type of the disorder.

When the tonsils are enlarged, and they are sometimes so swollen as to prevent the swallowing of liquids, a portion of what is drunken returns through the nose. We shall find them less sensitive than in simple angina, and their surface, although it may not exhibit well-marked patches of pseudo-membrane, not unfrequently presents a peculiar appearance. Their mucous envelope is so thickened, because of the injection of its capillaries, that the spots which are ulcerated appear indented or depressed beneath the surface. These ulcers in the diphtheria simplex are sometimes coated with a thin, pearly pellicle, and again with a pale-colored pus. The deposit exfoliates at times, and is again renewed. The ulcers vary in size from that of a millet seed to that of a split pea, and there may be from one to half-a-dozen or more of them upon either tonsil. In a few cases, I have known their margins to bleed at intervals from the onset of the attack. Sometimes the mucus expectorated will be of a rusty color; in more severe cases it will resemble the prune-juice expectoration of typhoid pneumonia. Usually, however, there is discharged from the throat a thick, yellowish, ash-colored, offensive, tenacious and elastic mucus, which varies in amount in proportion to the extent of epithelial surface involved in the inflammatory action. This source of irritation to the fauces not unfrequently gives rise to repeated retching, and sometimes to more obstinate vomiting.

The voice may become thickened by the narrowing of the parts about or above the glottis, but will not be hoarse and stridulous unless the lesion has encroached upon the larynx. The hoarseness is generally more marked during the febrile paroxysm. At a later period, the glands give external evidence of enlargement; the tonsils are more frequently swollen. Sometimes, however, the salivary glands, including the parotid, are greatly tumefied. What is peculiar to the disorder is, that this lesion, if it proceed to suppuration at all, is more prone to develop and discharge itself through the skin, than into the throat or the oral cavity. In some examples, the pus finds an exit through the meatus auditorius externus. In others, abscesses form behind the ears. We shall speak of this, however, under the head of sequelæ.

The Odor of the Breath.—Writers upon diphtheria, I am assured, have not laid sufficient stress upon this single symptom. You are aware that there is an odor or effluvia which is peculiar to measles, another to the small-pox, and a third to the typhoid fever. I believe the same is true of the disease in question. In diphtheria, this symptom is never wanting. It is pathognomonic, and is always present. There may be no membranous deposit visible, but the odor of the breath, or the perspiration, tells the story. This may be sufficiently strong to taint the whole atmosphere of the sick chamber, or you may be able to detect it in the breath only. In either case it is peculiar. It is, indeed, a species of signal which should warn you to qualify your prognosis. I cannot define or analyze this odor. You should familiarize yourselves with it at your earliest convenience. The cause for it is found in the perverted secretions from the mucous surfaces, especially those from about the throat and fauces. The blood being depraved and poisoned by the specific zymotic cause, the secretions elaborated by the epithelial glands are rendered abnormal in character, consistency and odor. The various exanthemata owe their individual origin and peculiar characteristics to the introduction into the blood of a specific virus, which, in due time, develops its own legitimate fruits. These fruits are the symptoms proper to each of the several diseases named. The odor pathognomonic of each is as directly referable to the toxicohæmic cause as is any other symptom evolved. Precisely similar causes, I apprehend, originate the odor of the breath in diphtheria. A little tact, experience, education in its recognition, may be of the greatest service to you as practitioners. It is of the utmost importance to be able to detect this insidious and treacherous affection at as early a date as possible, in order to anticipate and thwart its more serious development and consequences. Let me illustrate:

Case.—Three days ago I was called to visit a gentleman of thirty years, who had been ill for forty-eight hours. He had a febrile paroxysm each evening, which lasted into the night, and was accompanied by a species of delirium. He would awaken from a short and disturbed sleep considerably frightened, become exceedingly nervous, restless, then quite conscious, and afterward go off into a delirium again—sometimes make a speech to an imaginary audience, and again improvise poetry of no mean order of merit. During the remission, these cerebral symptoms were not present. The only suffering experienced was referred to the epigastrium. The pain was intermittent, colicky in nature, and relieved somewhat by eructations of flatus. He had anorexia, with no desire for drinks of any kind. Water tasted flat and insipid, as did also whatever he took into his mouth. His tongue was thickly coated with a whitish, granular-looking fur, through which the papillæ projected; its tip and margins were not of that fiery red hue which is a characteristic symptom of gastritis. Pulse 90, a little quick and irritable. But for a single symptom, I would have been compelled to diagnose the case as one of gastric, or bilious fever. This symptom was the peculiar odor of the breath, recognized immediately upon entering the room, on my first visit. Subsequent developments confirmed my conclusions. Thirty-six hours later, I found the throat somewhat inflamed, the tonsils slightly tumefied, and other characteristic signs of the diphtheria simplex cropping out here and there. This single symptom, therefore—the peculiar odor of the breath—enabled me not only to form a correct diagnosis, but to settle at once upon the plan of treatment most appropriate to the case. A day and a night were thus gained to its therapeutical management, which must have been lost had we waited for the throat symptoms to be developed, or prescribed for the relief of the more obvious tokens of a primary disorder in the stomach.

This is, therefore, a practical subject. I have known a physician to treat such cases, occurring in children, under the name and title of "gastric fever," with aconite, arsenicum, bryonia, chamomilla, nux vomica and kindred remedies, without the least curative result, for the simple reason that he did not recognize in the breath of the little sufferers this pathognomonic symptom of the diphtheria. Under these circumstances the more familiar medicines would prove powerless, because they were not specifically adapted to the cure of the actual lesion. It was not in their sphere, or within the range of their remedial action to accomplish so much.

The Coryza.—One of the first symptoms of this affection is a catarrhal disorder in the Schneiderian mucous membrane. You will be told that the patient has been seized with a cold in the head, or it may be that he has an attack of influenza. The secretion of the nostrils, like those of the throat, is changed in character. The nasal mucus is thin, yellowish-white in hue, at first scanty, afterwards profuse in amount. After some days it becomes acrid and pungent, excoriating the alæ nasi, and leaving a fiery red abrasion in its track, or wherever it touches the surface of the lips or cheeks. In the later stage, especially when the disease has assumed the more depraved type, it is corrosive, septic, disorganizing, destroying the soft parts with which it comes into contact, without pain. Excepting only snch cases as relapse from the milder into the more severe form of the disease, and those also which consist of a complication of diphtheria and scarlatina—which are always dangerous—the coryza is an earlier and more constant feature of the diphtheria simplex than of diphtheria maligna.

The acridity of the secretions not unfrequently produces such ulcerations of the nasal mucous membrane as to occasion a more or less troublesome hæmorrhage. When there is a predisposition to it in an hæmorrhagic diathesis, epistaxis may set in, even in the milder cases. In those which are of a more aggravated nature, it is sometimes an exceedingly troublesome symptom. Here at least two causes tend to make it alarming and intractable. The septic humors have broken in upon the organizing processes peculiar to the mucous tissue. Textural repairs are damaged by a morbid irritant from without. Beside this, the organizable fluid, the plasma, which is afforded by the circulation, is already depraved when furnished to the parts. The crasis of the blood, its capability of being organized by the cell-forces proper to the structure, is in part or entirely destroyed. The blood filters in a passive manner through the sub-mucous septa. Both these causes act and re-act, first to produce, and afterwards to repeat the attack of hæmorrhage.

The value of this symptom as an aid in prognosis can scarcely be estimated. Whenever it persists and is very troublesome, because of injury to adjacent parts, including the posterior nares, the alæ nasi, the lips, the cheeks, causing hæmorrhage, or suffusion of the eyes, there is good and sufficient reason for making a guarded prognosis. You should not commit yourselves unreservedly to the promise of a speedy cure, neither that the patient will always recover. The little fellow may be interested in his sports, running about the room, or even out of doors; the adult engaged with his daily duties; but if you shall find this symptom present in either class of patients, I charge you to institute such hygeinic precautions, and order such a treatment as shall be most suited to the case in point. Do not fail to realize that a few hours' delay may decide upon the fatal consequences of your neglect.

The Cough is subject to greater variations from a fixed standard than is almost any other symptom. If the epithelial disorganization shall extend into the larynx and trachea, it will be croupy, loud, ringing and sibilant, the sound produced being pitched upon a high and peculiar key. Aphonia, which is more or less complete, will also be present. If the bronchial mucous surfaces are the seat of the lesion, whether it be functional or organic, there will be less ringing, tension, and metallic sound than is characteristic of the laryngeal, or laryngo-tracheal cough. It is more sonorous, more base.

There may be cases in which the parenchymatous structure of the lungs is inflamed, and this will occasion a cough and expectoration similar to that of a legitimate pneumonia. Again, the cough may arise from prickling and tickling sensations in the fauces. At other times, more especially in cases of very delicate children and females, it will partake of nervous and hysterical characteristics. Sometimes there is a violent concussion with the cough, and the little patient will clasp both hands to his head, one over each ear, for the relief of a feeling of pressure, as if the head would burst open.

The cough is always a more troublesome symptom when

the attack of diphtheria supervenes upon one of whooping cough, measles, influenza, or pneumonia, and will, of course, be more or less modified by whatever disorder has immediately preceded it.

We may have frequent occasion to remark a decided aggravation of this symptom when an attempt is made to swallow liquids, more especially cold water, and also upon lying down. The character and severity of the cough will be modified by atmospheric vicissitudes. The patient, no matter how comfortably situated, will be certain to show an increased liability to take cold.

The Gastric Symptoms.—In this form of the diphtheria, a large proportion of cases suffer, either primarily or secondarily, from epigastric pain and disorder. When complaint is made of this symptom, prior to any visible throat affection, it is more than probable that kindred changes in texture and function are being experienced by the gastric mucous membrane. These changes may result in disorganization, giving rise to a form of ulcerative stomatitis, which may be confined entirely to that viscus, or propagated by continuity of surface to the pharynx and fauces. Or, the lesion may commence in the throat and travel downwards. The suffering experienced will be due in part to textural changes which have involved the functional sensibility, as well as the organic integrity of the inner coat of the stomach; and in part, also, to the perverted nature of the secretions which are swallowed into, or furnished by that organ. In case of pseudo-membranous deposits, upon its lining surface, we should anticipate a necessary disorder of function. The heteroplastic structure would differ in organization from the cylindrical epithelium which lines the superior portion of the gastric tubes. With the change of form in this, and the glandular cells also, which lie below, we shall certainly have a change in function. A severe blow would thus be aimed at the integrity of the digestive process. The stimulus of the presence of food, or other material, introduced into the stomach, would not call forth the production of the gastric juice, for that solvent can only be elaborated by a particular species of organ, one which has been constructed with especial reference to this particular end. The tough and half-organized fluids which are yielded by the supra-diaphragmatic and respiratory mucous membranes, in an attack of diphtheria, and which a young child does not know, and cannot be taught how to expectorate, are as indigestible as a chip of sole-leather.

These physiological remarks explain the cause of the anorexia, as well as of the absence of considerable thirst, which are generally most decided when the gastric symptoms predominate. An early and obstinate vomiting of ingesta may be due to the same cause. I have previously indicated the manner in which the gastric disorder is to be identified as a prominent symptom of the diphtheria simplex. If there is present a sudden and extreme prostration, the source of which does not lie in some exhaustive discharge, as, for example, a hæmorrhage, a profuse secretion of mucus from the respiratory passages, or of albumen with the urine, and the breath has the characteristic odor of the disease in question, the significance of this disorder will be manifest. The local lesion, the congestion, the ulceration, the pseudo-membranous deposits, may each and all occur within the stomach, the throat being secondarily, or not at all affected.

The Eruption.—There are, of course, exceptions to the rule, but the diphtheritic eruption appears to be much more common to the diphtheria simplex than to the diphtheria maligna. Why this is so, we cannot tell. It may be that this type of the disease is rendered more mild for the reason that the morbid irritant finds vent at the cutaneous surface. Where the eruption is entirely wanting, the attack is apt to develop into a more severe and dangerous form of the complaint. A modification in severity may be due to a relief of internal surfaces. Where it comes out freely, the remaining symptoms appear modified thereby. If, however, the disease is complicated with rubeola, or scarlatina, the case will be very different.

Here a profuse eruption might indicate an extreme degree of danger, for it is not true, as is generally held, that in scarlatina the danger is lessened in proportion as a copious eruption is made to appear upon the skin.

We cannot fix precisely upon the latent period characterizing the duration of time between the inception of the diphtheritic cause and the appearance of the eruption. Its period of *incubation* varies in different cases. Sometimes the patient will have been ill for a week, with nightly exacerbations and daily remissions of fever, and other symptoms of the disease, before any sign of the eruption has appeared. Or, it may be the first symptom indicative of ill health, the earliest to call the attention of the nurse or patient to any bodily ailment. Not unfrequently, it will be entirely wanting until subsequent to the decline of the other symptoms, when it will appear for a few hours, or a day at farthest, and then decline. Again, it will show itself early, then fade out entirely, and, by-and-by, it may be in a week, or ten days later, return, in the same manner as the secondary eruption of the scarlet fever occasionally does. As you would expect, a sudden retrocession of the eruption in diphtheria, as well as in the true exanthemata, may give rise to alarming symptoms. It would be *malpraxis* to employ any means which should tend to its translation from the free cutaneous to the internal mucous surfaces, since these may be already endangered by the most serious lesions, both of structure and of function.

The eruption, which appears in the form of a rash, is sometimes of a dark or purplish color, bearing a close resemblance to that of measles, at others, bright and scarlet, as in the scarlet fever. I have known several cases to be mistaken for and treated as rubeola; while it is no unusual occurrence for the practitioner to be so misled by the particular hue of the rash as to pronounce it the scarlatina. Indeed, the eruption in diphtheria would seem to be a sort of "cross" between that peculiar to each of the two diseases last named, partaking of the characteristics of both, yet sometimes more nearly alike in appearance to the one than to the other. There is no desquamation of cuticle after genuine diphtheria. In certian epidemics, it has an erysipelatous look. Such a type of the disorder is of very grave nature, being always more prone to run into the diphtheria maligna. It may be limited, as regards the extent of surface covered by it, to the face and neck, the body, or the upper and lower extremities. In a considerable number of cases, I have remarked that it came out most freely, and, indeed, exclusively upon the back. This item, in very mild attacks, will sometimes be of service in forming a correct diagnosis.

The Disorder of the Urinary Function.—Albuminuria is a concomitant of the diphtheria, of which we shall have occasion to speak more particularly in another place. In the present connection, it must suffice to remark that it is a less constant symptom in this than in the malignant variety of diphtheria. Here there is every reason to believe the organism suffers less severely from the operation of the blood-poison. The excretory functions are less seriously disordered. The urine will sometimes vary in quantity from the natural standard, becoming scanty in amount, and voided at long intervals. Its quality will also be changed, in proportion to the height of the fever, the dryness of the skin, and the severity of the bilious and gastric disorder. Under these circumstances, it will be thick, dark-colored, and offensive, especially upon being allowed to stand for a little while; or it may be high-colored, hot, and somewhat acrid in nature, or turbid and ropy. As in the pyrexiæ generally, the proportion of the urates contained in this fluid is said to be considerably increased in the diphtheria simplex, showing a characteristic detritus of the nitrogenized tissues.

The presence of albumen in the urine is remarked in cases of every grade of severity, from the mildest to the most severe. In Dr. Condie's experience, albuminuria is present in not more than one-fourth the cases of diphtheria met with. We may sometimes detect albumen by means of appropriate tests, in the earlier stages of the diphtheria, but usually it is a more decided symptom of an advanced period of the disease. It is said to be present in a majority of those cases which prove fatal, but is not, therefore, necessarily a fatal symptom.

Here are two specimens of albuminous urine which have been voided by patients ill with diphtheria. One of them has the diphtheria simplex, the other the diphtheria maligna. In the former sample, the patient having been sick for ten days, there is but the merest trace of albumen visible upon the application of the ordinary tests, heat and nitric acid. In that afforded by the diphtheria maligna, you will remark the milky, opalescent hue of the urine, as contained in the bottle, and also that both these tests occasion a dense precipitate of albumen in the test-tube.

The date of the commencement of the albuminuria is reported to be characterized, in many instances, by an increased degree of fever. Not unfrequently, the patient has seemed to convalesce—the fever to have declined—when suddenly, and for no appreciable reason of a local nature, there is a relapse. The febrile character is resumed, re-appearing in an aggravated form. The earlier symptoms return, and with increased severity. Such untoward changes are believed to indicate the advent of a marked disorder in the excretory function of the kidneys. Because of structural changes in the glandular epithelium lining the uriniferous tubes, the secerning process is deranged. The plasma filters away, when only the salts of the urine should have been selected from out the contents of the little capillary vessels; and the irrigating waters from the tufts of Malphigii are made to carry off the organizable element, thus impoverishing the blood.

If, with the suppression of the sensible perspiration, the flow of urine shall be entirely checked, other symptoms will be added to the already lengthened list. Articular rheumatism frequently presents itself as supplementary upon a retention of urine. If, along with this cause, the patient be predisposed to rheumatism, or the weather and surroundings be favorable to its production, this addition to his suffering will be an almost certain result. It will prove a wise precaution on the part of the physician, even in the milder cases, to know that the urinary product is voided, either in a natural or artificial manner, at least once in every twenty-four hours. You will understand that an excess of urea may minister to a retention of urine, by causing a disproportion between its solid and liquid constituents.

Of the Local and General Debility.—This form of the diphtheria, as the diphtheria maligna, is characterized by a degree of prostration, which, at first thought, is not easily accounted for. The little patient does not appear very ill. He may be running about the house, and show but few of the symptoms we have enumerated—even these being felt in a very mild degree. But, after a few hours, or days at the farthest, have elapsed, he makes complaint, in the Western vernacular, of feeling "powerful weak." He has not been the victim of any exhausting discharge, which might drain away the nutritive resources. Has had no hæmorrhage, no profuse perspiration, or expectoration, and no diarrhœa.

There is no great waste of albumen in forming the pseudomembrane—for, in this class of cases, it may be almost entirely wanting,—and no albuminuria.

What, then, is the source of the debility? We must refer it to a disordered and depraved innervation. When I come to speak of the nature of diphtheria, you will understand in what manner the patient's strength is sapped by the direct impression of the poison, which circulates with the blood, upon the nerve-centres, both of animal and of organic life. The virus finds the nervous system extremely susceptible to its toxical influence. It poisons the very fountain and source of animal dynamics. It aims a blow at the precise point in which the organism is most vulnerable.

The consequences are manifested in a train of local and general symptoms, indicative of disordered innervation. Patients will tell you that a few hours' illness has caused them to feel as if they had undergone a severe and protracted indisposition. Indeed, you will sometimes be questioned concerning the cause of this positive prostration, by those who cannot understand why a common cold, or influenza, should have weakened them to such a degree. I have frequently seen the most robust children, and adults also, thus suddenly stripped of strength sufficient for locomotion. During the febrile remission, the little one, suffering apparently, from but a slight nasal catarrh, sometimes totters about as if he were intoxicated. His legs are very weak, and his arms may be almost helpless, from sheer lack of the motor force which should be supplied to them.

In some cases, there will be anæsthesia of the surface of one or another of the extremities. This paralysis of the sensory filaments, is, however, rarely met with in this form of the complaint. The nerves of special sense are liable to attack. Disorders of vision are by no means infrequent. The patient is much annoyed with an inability to read—cannot distinguish the letters on a printed page. All is a blur, and the characters are jumbled together without order. Writing is impossible, for the lines run together, and there is great confusion in the brain while attempting it. The hearing is impaired. This may be explained by the fact that the inflammation of the throat and fauces has traveled, by continuity of surface, along the Eustachian tube, leaving its earlier or more remote consequences to derange the function of the auditory filaments. Or, it may be due to a direct impression of the virus upon the nerve which presides over the sense of hearing. The other varieties of special sense may be, either directly or indirectly, implicated in the disordered action.

LECTURE II.

DIPHTHERIA SIMPLEX CONTINUED.—DIFFERENTIAL DIAGNOSIS OF.—*From Tonsillitis.—From Ulcerative Stomatitis.—From Rubeola.—From Scarlatina.—From Epidemic Influenza.*—PROGNOSIS.—EPIDEMIC AND ENDEMIC PECULIARITIES.—*Discrepancies in Mortality Reports.—How they are to be reconciled.*

DIPHTHERIA MALIGNA.—*Case.—The Fever.—The Cerebral Symptoms.—The exudation upon the Throat and Fauces.—Varieties of.—The Larynx and Trachea.—The Nasal Symptoms.—Various localities in which the Pseudo-Membrane is deposited.—Relative frequency of, upon the Throat, Tonsils, Palate, etc.—The Hæmorrhagic Symptoms.—Case.*

GENTLEMEN:—

DIFFERENTIAL DIAGNOSIS.—The differential diagnosis of the Diphtheria Simplex is more easily made out than is that of the Diphtheria Maligna. The diseases with which the former are more likely to be confounded, are tonsillitis, ulcerative stomatitis, rubeola, scarlatina, and epidemic influenza.

From Tonsillitis.—Tonsillitis, or Quinsy, occurs most frequently in those persons, whether old or young, who have inherited a predisposition to it. In such subjects, the tonsils are unusually large in health. Any of the more ordinary exciting causes of the phlegmasiæ serve to develop an inflammation in them. They become very painful, swollen, and of a bright scarlet hue. These symptoms are marked from the onset of the attack. The throat is the first thing complained of. The fever almost invariably commences with a chill, and, in severe cases, there is little or no remission until suppuration has taken place. Where the tumefaction is finally resolved away, the bad odor of the breath, as found in diphtheria, is altogether wanting. It may be sour, hot, unpleasant, and feverish, but it is not diphtheritic. Where pus is really formed and discharged into the mouth or throat, the breath becomes more offensive and putrid, resembling that of malignant scarlatina.

In my own experience, those who are most predisposed to quinsy, are not the most liable to suffer from attacks of diphtheria. Indeed, where I find parents more than usually solicitous lest their children should be seized with it—because of their having had frequent attacks of tonsillitis—it is my habit to calm their fears, by assuring them of a probable exemption for this very reason. The same is true of the croup, as I shall tell you presently.

In tonsillitis, the surface of the mucous membrane covering the amygdalæ is scarlet, smooth and shining. The little sulci are almost or quite obliterated by the swelling. In the diphtheria simplex, the indentations are yet visible, notwithstanding the increased size of the organ, while the surface of the enveloping tissue is darker in hue, and dotted here and there with the irritable-looking ulcers, or the pearly pellicular coating of which I have spoken.

Tonsillitis will be recognized by the careful physician as a local disorder, affecting the tonsils primarily, and the general system in a secondary manner. Diphtheria, in either form of the disease, is essentially constitutional, and may or may not be developed locally.

From Ulcerative Stomatitis.—This form of sore-mouth rarely exists as an acute affection. If accompanied by fever at all, it is of the continued type. There is no cough, no eruption, no evidence of sudden and extreme prostration, and no marked disorder of innervation, at any period of the disease. The ulcerated spots have a less irritable look, their edges are less serrated and vascular, while the solution of continuity does not dip so deeply into the oral mucous membrane. The odor is not peculiar.

In their essential nature, these two diseases are very different. Ulcerative stomatitis arises from a depraved plasma, which is incapable of healthy histogenetic organization. Here, there is no new tissue formed after the old type; neither is there a new one constructed at all. In these particular spots, the function of nutrition is a failure. In the diphtheria, the blood is as certainly poisoned, but wherever the ulcers appear, we shall find the evidence of an attempt at organization. The proper epithelial structure may not indeed be renewed, but we shall discover that the tissue-making process has not entirely aborted.

There has been what we may term a false conception. This disposition in diphtheria to the formation of a pseudo-membrane upon the tongue, the lips, the gums, cheeks, or fauces, is not present in any form of the stomatitis, whether it be follicular, apthous, or gangrenous.

From Rubeola.—In measles, the period of incubation is in general well-marked. In most cases, the eruption appears on the fourth day. In diphtheria, there seems no definite time in which the cause operates within the organism to the development of its characteristic external symptoms—at least we do not know what that latent period is. The eruption may appear on the fourth day, or not until a very much later period, or, in many cases, never appear upon the body at all.

In measles, the minute pimples coalesce into blotches, which are of a dark, mottled, and sometimes, as the eruption fades, of almost a mahogany color. The striking peculiarity of this rubeoloid eruption is that the blotches form themselves into the shape of a crescent or a horse-shoe. In diphtheria, the eruption is more of a raspberry hue, distinct and scattered, and does not form into the definite shapes which are characteristic of the measles.

The catarrhal symptoms are the chief source of deception,

where these two disorders are confounded. In measles, the vitiated secretions from the mucous membrane lining the nares and bronchial passages, are less acrid and irritating than in diphtheria. The discharges from the nostrils do not excoriate the alæ nasi, the upper lip and the cheeks; neither is there that sense of rawness in the windpipe as when the lining surface of the respiratory tubes is involved in diphtheria.

The odor of the breath and of the body in each case, is as different as day and night. I can no more define this difference, than I can define that which so distinctly separates in our minds the perfume of the rose from that of the violet. There is only one avenue through which you can learn to recognize this differential sign between the measles and diphtheria—by your own sense of olfaction.

In measles, the accompanying fever is of the continued type, and declines into a remittent upon the appearance of the eruption. In the diphtheria simplex, it is most frequently remittent from the commencement of the attack, and the type is not changed in the least by the rash, no matter whether it come sooner or later, or if not at all.

If we except the rheumatism, the sequelæ of the two diseases are very different. Pulmonary complaints are more liable to follow measles than the diphtheria; while after the acute stage of the latter, there is a liability to glandular swellings, and nervous derangements, in regard either of sensibility or of motion, or of both these together.

From Scarlatina.—There are but two forms of the scarlatina with which this variety of diphtheria is liable to be confounded, the scarlatina simplex and the scarlatina anginosa. There are, however, certain points of difference which may aid us to diagnose the diphtheria from either of these. These concern the fever, the appearance and decline of the eruption, the throat affection, and the nervous symptoms and sequelæ.

In every case of scarlatina, no matter how mild in degree, the heat of skin which is found in its earlier stages, is remarkable. This heat usually continues without abatement until the eruption makes its appearance. Or, if the latter be wanting, we still find a characteristic increase of temperature, which does not change very materially until the period has elapsed during which the rash should have run its course. In the great majority of examples of scarlatina, as in rubeola, there is no remission of the fever until the rash has broken out. The little patient may lie for twenty-four, thirty-six, or even for forty-eight or more hours, without any decline in the fever. When the rash appears, the surplus heat seems to have, in a measure, departed.

The fever in scarlatina does not entirely leave, as in most eruptive diseases, upon the appearance of the exanthem. Its type becomes remittent or irregular, instead of continued. This change is due to a species of critical discharge, designed for the relief of the general organism, of which there are at least four varieties, viz: that from the skin, the alimentary mucous membrane, the kidneys, and the nervous system. The breaking out of the rash, brings relief through the skin as an excretory outlet for vitiated and suppressed secretions, which are thus set free by a more or less profuse diaphoresis. If this species of safety-valve remain closed, the digestive or respiratory surfaces become the seat of the eruptive lesion, in which case, a thin, watery, and more or less profuse diarrhœa, or a copious expectoration of catarrhal mucus, will ultimately result.

Or the compensatory function of excretion by the kidneys may be enlisted for the relief of the excess of febrile action. Diuresis is a frequent symptom of scarlatina at the period of the disease of which we are speaking. Structural changes in the kidneys, as in Bright's disease, albuminuria, and even dropsy, result from this excess of duty, in striving to perform their own function in addition to that which is proper to the skin.

In the diphtheria simplex, there is a daily and nightly remission and exacerbation of the fever throughout the course of the complaint.

There are cases of scarlatina, however, in which the febrile symptoms either subside entirely, or are greatly modified, before the rash has showed itself upon the surface. But these are to be regarded as exceptions to the général rule, and are in themselves instructive. In scarlatina, when this condition of things happens, you should be on your guard, for there is great danger of convulsions. The tardy advent of the eruption, and the cooling off of the skin, portend the most serious consequences to the nervous system. Here, the more ordinary of the three outlets of which we have spoken is closed, and the whole specific disease-force is correllated to that of the nervous system.

Not so in the disease whose peculiarities we are studying. The eruption appears to bear but little relation to the height and severity, or duration of the febrile symptoms. It may appear at an early date of the disease, or not until very late, or indeed fail to appear; and yet the daily cycles in the fever go on as if its legitimate course were being accomplished. Its suppression, or its re-percussion, does not increase the liability to convulsions. The poison may concentrate its force upon the blood and the solids, may so derange the function of innervation as to give rise to anasthæsia, or even to a super-sensitiveness of the surface, may produce paralysis of the muscles, incipient amaurosis, or even deafness, but will not occasion genuine convulsions.

Valleix, a French authority, recognizes another diagnostic symptom separating the scarlatina and diphtheria. In the former, the decline of the eruption is characterized by desquamation of the cuticle, while that of the latter is not. This is a very important distinction, and may serve in part to explain the extreme degree of debility which follows a rapid and general exfoliation of the epidermis. This drain upon the system produces effects which are kindred in nature to the sapping of the strength by the loss of albumen in the formation of the false membrane, and in the albuminuria of genuine diphtheria.

In the anginose form of scarlatina, the tonsils are indeed swollen, but their color is scarlet, and their surface smooth and shining. Sometimes they are whitened with a filmy, transparent layer of mucus, which appears, at first sight, to be organized. This appearance is deceptive. The deposit will be readily distinguished from the more distinct and deeper seated ulceration which is found upon the tonsils in the diphtheria simplex. Trousseau, in his Clinical Lectures, says that, in diphtheria, the swelling of the cervical glands, which is sometimes so enormous as to extend beyond the jaw, is altogether out of proportion to the intensity of the faucial affection.

Death rarely anticipates the formation of the pseudo-membranous deposit, or of the diphtheritic ulcer in milder cases of the diphtheria, at some point upon the mucous surfaces. In scarlatina, however, it may, and often does happen, before either the throat symptoms or the eruption are present in any very marked degree.

Paralytic affections, either of the sensory or motor filaments, or of both these together, is a not unfrequent accompaniment and sequel of diphtheria. Even the milder cases are liable to be thus complicated. Such symptoms are but seldom witnessed in any form of the scarlatina.

From Epidemic Influenza.—The diagnosis from a prevalent influenza is more readily made out. The acridity of the nasal and bronchial secretions, the peculiar affection of the tonsils and fauces, the pungent heat of the skin, the type of the fever, the sudden prostration of the patient's strength, and the nervous phenomena which characterize the diphtheria simplex, will serve to distinguish it from the most violent and intractable species of influenza.

PROGNOSIS.—As there is no disease with which we are acquainted, which is more insidious in its approach and development, or treacherous in its very nature, so there are none in which your prognosis should be more guarded. The mildest attack of diphtheria simplex may result unfavorably. The seeds of the terrible scourge may lie for a time quite latent in the organism, ready, by-and-by, to bloom and bear their fatal fruit. This type of the disease may merge, either gradually or suddenly, into its more malignant form. Every case is liable to such a termination.

It is a cruel thing for a physician to take advantage of the natural solicitude of parents and friends, lest their families should be smitten by this destroyer. You need not announce the probability, but you may tell such of them as are sufficiently intelligent to appreciate the explanation, of the possibility of danger, and that the greatest care is requisite in order to ensure a certain recovery.

Not unfrequently, almost the only signs of the diphtheria simplex which remain, will be the acrid coryza, the irritated nostrils, the sore and excoriated lips. These symptoms, the effect of perverted secretions, appear of little significance, in themselves considered. But to the intelligent pathologist, they evidence a disorder in the blood, which is liable at any time to develop and unfold the most serious consequences. Physicians have been known to promise that trifling examples of this kind should recover in a day or two, when the sequel proves them to have died, in some cases at an early, in others at a later period, and from a more aggravated form of the disease.

In the diphtheria simplex, the danger will be proportioned to the type and character of the epidemic. In certain localities and seasons, almost every case proves fatal; again, almost all attacked recover. If the symptoms are complicated with scarlatina, measles, or erysipelas—all of which diseases, it has been observed, are apt to prevail in one neighborhood at the same time—we shall anticipate serious consequences, and be led to a more careful prognosis.

The nervous symptoms and sequelæ will also afford us some criterion of the gravity of the attack. While they persist, we may not feel that our patient is entirely free from danger. An impending paralysis in less vital parts may fall upon those which are most vulnerable. The brain, the heart, or the lungs, may suddenly become powerless, and life itself extinct. The dilated pupil, which is almost a pathognomonic symptom of this disease, will sometimes warn you not to promise an exemption from fatal consequences to the cerebro-spinal centre.

The extensive suppuration, seen in the formation of abscesses about the throat, and in various parts of the body, may subtract from the chances of recovery by draining away the nutritive resources of an organism which is already enfeebled by disease. Post-diphtheritic abscesses, if numerous, will cause you no slight measure of anxiety, for the simple reason that it is impossible to anticipate their situation, their size, or the serious consequences which may ultimately result from them.

Epidemic and Endemic Peculiarities.—There is but one method of reconciling the conflicting reports of physicians concerning the results of their treatment of the diphtheria. One will tell you, for example, that, in all, he has treated some sixty, seventy, or even one hundred or more cases, with, it it may be, but one or two deaths. Another, from a different section of country, questions if this report is not greatly exaggerated. He has been much less successful, and lost say one-third of his cases of diphtheria. A third insists, that in his experience, it is quite an easy matter to bring every example of the disease to a successful issue. He relies upon the simpler and better-known remedies, as aconite, belladonna, and mercurius solubilis, and believes it within their curative range to control it entirely. Others, again, place but little confidence in these means, because they have succeeded best with a very different class of remedies.

That method of reconciliation lies in a recognition of the *varying character of the complaint, as met with in different localities and seasons.* In one neighborhood, its type may be of a mild nature, which permits almost every case to terminate favorably. In another, the opposite is true. Local or epidemic causes, or both these, have given a greater gravity to the symptoms, and imprinted a fatal type upon them. The simpler remedies are of slight avail. Others are certainly called for, but despite these, and the utmost skill of the practitioner, multitudes die. In one locality, almost every case of the diphtheria simplex will be marked by a characteristic eruption. In other parts of the country there are experienced physicians, familiar with the disease, and who have gone through one or more of its epidemics without ever yet having seen the diphtheritic eruption.

As it prevails this year, a majority of those who are seized will complain of abnormal sensations at the epigastrium, and later in the course of the affection, almost without exception, of a more or less troublesome diarrhœa. In the very next epidemic, these symptoms may be absent, and the local evidence of disorder be transferred to the pituitary membrane, or to some other portion of the respiratory mucous surfaces, leaving the alimentary sympathies unimpaired. If the prevailing type of disease is typhoid or adynamic in character, cases of diphtheria occurring at the same time will be modified thereby. If the fevers of a particular locality are most of them intermittent, the miasmatic cause may impress some of its paroxysmal characteristics upon the epidemic diphtheria. If the eruptive diseases, as scarlatina, rubeola, or erysipelas, are prevalent, the malignancy of the diphtheria may be of a more decided character. Local causes, as impure air, or water, or food, will also exercise their influence in varying the type of this disease.

All of these qualifications, together with numerous sequelæ, of which we shall take occasion to speak in the proper place, will tend to reconcile us to discrepancies in the therapeutical verdict of our medical brethren. It will also serve to explain why any one of us may discover that he has been far more successful in the management of the disease at one time than at another.

DIPHTHERIA MALIGNA.

Case.—Thomas G., aged five years, became my patient two days since. The history of this case is as follows: The little fellow had a severe chill in the evening, which was followed by a burning fever. This fever lasted some hours, and finally subsided, in the early morning, into a remission, but without any flow of the sensible perspiration. The heat of skin was very marked—the nurse says he was so hot that it was like touching a heated stove to put her hand upon him. As it abated, he commenced to complain of terrible pains in the limbs and back; was restless, fretful, nervous, inclined to roll himself about from side to side of the bed, and would cry for the most trifling cause. His appetite disappeared; there was slight nausea, and considerable thirst, especially during the hot stage of the fever. Tongue coated a yellowish-brown in color, as in the early stage of typhoid fever. He was flighty: had a wild look, starting suddenly out of sleep, and gazing wildly at the door, the stove, and about the room. Once, he called the attention of the nurse to a great collection of eyes around one of the chairs—"more eyes than he ever saw before." Pupils dilated, eyes first glaring and then languid in expression. Bowels normal, urine ditto. No cough. Throat much congested, and tonsils swollen. Complains of stiffness in the muscles of the neck. Says he felt inclined all the day previous to hold his head bent to the right, in order to relieve the pain and soreness in the muscles of that side of the neck. These symptoms continued throughout the day.

In the evening of the second day, the fever returned with increased severity, but the cold stage was wanting. The extreme heat lasted some eight hours, and then declined as before, without diaphoresis. During the paroxysm, his nervous symptoms did not vary essentially from those reported for the night previous.

The next morning I was called to see him. Great heat of surface. Pulse 120, rather weak, irritable, quick and jerking. Whole palate and tonsils considerably swollen, both externally and internally. Deglutition difficult, on account of the soreness of the throat. A large sized patch of thick wash-leather deposit is visible upon the right tonsil, and another upon the mucous membrane of the pharynx. This latter appears to extend for a considerable distance in a downward direction. It is attached very firmly to the sub-mucous tissue beneath. The breath is fœtid and diphtheritic. Respiration but slightly impaired—a little thickened, but not croupy. There is a slight cough, with evident dryness of the bronchial mucous membrane. He expectorates, from the throat only, a yellowish, tenacious mucus, which at times is sufficient to nauseate him and to occasion retching. Is very weak and prostrate. Has no appetite, but would drink largely were it not for a dread of swallowing anything whatever. Cold drinks, especially, occasion him much suffering and dysphagia. His face is pale, the upper lip of a bluish cast. The nostrils are dilated widely with each inspiration. They are not, however, excoriated, although evidently much stuffed and occluded. He cannot breathe with his mouth closed. Has an anxious, imploring look. His mind is, however, perfectly clear. Physical exploration does not reveal any abnormal chest-symptoms.

In the evening.—Heat of skin has declined. There is no visible eruption upon the body or extremities. Pulse 130, with the same irritable characteristics as in the morning. The tumefaction of the tonsils and adjacent parts much increased. The patch of false membrane upon the right tonsil has extended so as almost to cover the entire organ, while upon the left one, there is a deposit of a like nature of the size of the thumb-nail. The superior compartment of the pharynx is coated with this abnormal exudation. There is great difficulty in swallowing and in breathing. His nostrils are almost entirely closed, while from them there exudes, in considerable amount, a species of acrid and bloody mucus. He cannot breathe in a recumbent posture. His little chest heaves with each respiratory act. He coughs but seldom, and this to dislodge an excess of mucus, which seems to oppress the air-passages. That which he can be persuaded to throw from his mouth, is yellowish, purulent-looking, and in it are contained hard masses of membranous substance, the edges of which are sometimes streaked with blood. Both the matter expectorated and the breath are of a very offensive odor. He is exceedingly prostrate, with a cool skin. His mind totters, and his vital forces run low—he is evidently sinking. We shall discuss the more prominent symptoms of this case separately, as has already been done in treating of the diphtheria simplex.

The Fever.—In idiopathic diphtheria of the more aggravated type, most attacks are ushered in either by a decided chill, or by rigors, which are followed by the pungent heat of the skin and general perturbation of which I have spoken. It is rarely, however, that the cold stage is repeated. The heat continues for some hours, and in the worst cases abates but little in violence before the advent of another paroxysm. The remission is less decided than in the diphtheria simplex. The type of the fever is less distinct also. There is frequently a paroxysm in the morning, and another at evening. The fit is accompanied by a delirium, which, in general, is not violent, but passive in nature, with muttering and incoherent speech, sudden startings from sleep, with staring of the eyes, and non-recognition of his parents, trembling of the hands and limbs, and evident debility. During the remission, however slight, this symptom may or may not disappear.

In a few cases, the degree of fever, when compared with the severity of the throat-symptoms, will be very slight indeed. Here, it will not afford a good criterion of the gravity of the attack. You should examine the throat, the pulse, the general prostration, in order to measure its severity.

In most examples of the diphtheria maligna, the pulse is considerably accelerated. In this, it resembles that of scarlatina. It will not only be more frequent, but rapid, irritable, and sometimes thread-like and wiry. One might, by straining a point somewhat, style it a nervous pulse, so evident is it that the nervous system is chiefly affected. Its frequency and volume will vary somewhat during the remission of the fever. In the exacerbation, you would expect to find the relative number of its beats increased. While this irritability persists, you will remember that it is not safe to regard your patients as quite out of danger.

Anorexia is almost always present. The tongue is coated with a thick granular fur, of a yellowish-white color. The sense of taste is deranged, and the patient has no desire for food, were it possible for him to swallow most easily. The thirst is proportioned to the height of the fever, and the degree of irritation or inflammation of the gastric mucous membrane. In later stages, as the fever declines, even where the throat-symptoms are of a very aggravated nature, the appetite returns, and sometimes becomes excessive. I remember one very severe case of diphtheritic croup, in which my little patient seized hold upon and ate heartily of some water-crackers, not a quarter of an hour before his death. His strength had become suddenly increased to an almost superhuman degree, his appetite tormenting, and when his eye chanced to fall upon a plate of crackers, he insisted upon having them, and, sitting upright in bed, devoured them, even while he was dying.

The Cerebral Symptoms.—In a majority of examples of the diphtheria maligna, when the fever declines, as it is prone to do, if the case do not prove fatal after one or two days, the mental faculties become remarkably clear. The patient sits upright in bed, with a mature but distressed look, weighing every little circumstance about him with the coolness of a genuine philosopher. If the dyspnœa is not very marked, and articulation be possible, he may even inquire concerning the source of alarm to his parents and friends. Or, he may be impressed from the first with the probability of his death, and turn to moralizing, or to a pathetic leave-taking of those within hearing, whenever he ventures to speak. In some malignant cases, this is a most trying symptom.

I remember one little fellow who asked to be carried to the window that he might look out upon the snow. His mother held him as he desired. He asked her to wipe away the frost from the pane, that he might see. She took her handkerchief to comply, and, sooner than I can relate the incident, the vital spark had fled. In another case, a boy of six years, who had been ill with the disease only thirty-six hours, raised himself in the bed, and exclaiming, "Ma, how dark it is growing!"

died in an instant, and without the least struggle. Such a sudden and unlooked-for event may be attributed to poisoning of the nerve-centres, and sometimes to a mechanical obstruction to the free circulation of blood through the right side of the heart. In either case, you will not fail to remark the acuteness of the mental faculties up to the very moment of dissolution. As in the later stages of phthisis pulmonalis, the eye will flash a brighter light, and the mental perceptions be quickened, so in malignant diphtheria we sometimes find the light of life to burn more brilliantly just before going out.

Where the glands about the throat are greatly swollen, the brain symptoms are of a very different order. The increased size and tumefaction of these organs interferes, by mechanical pressure, with the free circulation of the blood to and from the head, through the cervical vessels. There is an increased liability to cerebral congestion. The little patient becomes either suddenly, or it may be more gradually, oblivious to external stimulii. He breathes stertorously, and lapses into a comatose state, death resulting, finally, in much the same manner as in malignant scarlatina.

The Throat and Fauces.—In most cases, the throat at first appears congested, and of a color that varies with the gravity of the remaining symptoms. In less malignant attacks, the faucial mucous membrane is of a light mahogany hue, shaded off into scarlet. In the most aggravated form it may have an erysipelatous look, or appear of a dark cranberry color. The discoloration is generally diffused over the tonsils, the velum palati, the uvula, and the superior part of the pharynx, extending as far down as one can see. The peculiar deposition may be abundant or scanty in amount. A very slight deposit at first, may be followed, at a later period, by an abundant exudation. The method of its organization varies. It may begin to form in small patches, which are at first quite distinct, but which extend more or less rapidly, and by-and-by coalesce, so as to curtain the entire faucial cavity. Or, the spots may remain separate and distinct from each other throughout the whole course of the disease. When this is the case, it is remarked there is an increased liability to a deep-seated erosion and sloughing of the sub-mucous structures. In some very malignant attacks, the phagadenic ulceration occurring upon the tonsils is so disorganizing as to dip down into and destroy, it may be, the entire organ.

I have treated a case in which the veil of the left palate was pierced, and an orifice resembling the foramen ovale in the fœtal heart, resulted from this cause. It sometimes happens, indeed, that the whole velum palati is destroyed, and patients recover, with an infirmity of the voice. At other times, the corrosive poison has been known to eat away the soft palate, or the uvula, neither of which organs can be afterwards restored.

Again, there will be a simultaneous deposition of pseudo-membrane over the entire throat. At one visit you may find the faucial mucous membrane slightly congested, of a mahogany hue, with no appearance of the peculiar exudation. A few hours later, there is not a spot upon its surface which is not covered by it. This membrane, so rapidly formed, is at first ash-colored, opaque, thick, and afterwards of a dark brown or blackish cast. The odor varies with these changes, degenerating from a marked diphtheritic to a gangrenous taint. The deposit may appear more or less thoroughly organized. Sometimes it is pultaceous, slimy, or it may have a curd-like, or a creamy appearance. Dr. Lord compares this kind of deposit to an oval slice of ice-cream, which is sunken more than half its thickness into the mucous membrane.

One peculiarity is conceded to be characteristic of the early formation of the pseudo-membrane—that it is in general easily detached from the mucous membrane, to which it adheres by very delicate filaments, and is soon succeeded by a new deposit, which takes the place of the old one. As the case progresses, the exudation becomes more thoroughly organized, thicker, and more tenacious. Sometimes there will be found a dense, compact, wash-leather-like deposit, which adheres more firmly to the subjacent tissue, and which, if it be detached, will leave a bleeding surface behind it. It is not uncommon to find this membrane several lines in thickness, having the appearance of numerous layers of organized plasma superimposed, the one upon the other. It may form into shreds or strings, which hang down into the pharynx, extend into the larynx or trachea, or are suspended from the nose, the mouth, or the external ear. Some authorities say, that in a majority of cases of the diphtheria maligna, we shall discover the abnormal deposit, by means of an appropriate speculum, to be located at the bottom of the meatus auditorius externus. As a rule, the membrane will dislodge itself before the sixth day. When cast off spontaneously, it is seldom re-formed again.

Deglutition will be difficult in proportion as the tonsils and adjacent parts are swollen, and as the lesion has involved the muscular contractility of the fauces and pharynx. The swelling of the tonsils is, in general, so marked, and the passage so occluded by the diphtheritic false membrane and the stringy mucus, which is present in large quantities, that it is very difficult for the patient to swallow either solids or cold drinks. Cold water, placed in the mouth, will sometimes almost set him into convulsions. He cannot drink it. Warm drinks, on the contrary, are less harmful and more easily passed into the stomach. Drinks of every variety, however, are apt to be returned in great part, and violently, through the nostrils. For this reason, it will sometimes be quite impossible to administer your remedies in cold water as a vehicle.

In certain epidemics, the first symptom observed will be a severe pain in the ear, which, from its not yielding to the more ordinary means of relief, attracts the attention through its very persistency. Again, and more particularly in those predisposed to neuralgia, or some form of rheumatism, a slight swelling of the submaxillary glands may occasion the most extreme suffering in one or both sides of the neck, which is increased by the least jar or movement of the body, and is finally relieved only when the proper throat symptoms are unmistakably developed.

Besides the enlargement of the tonsils, there is usually a swelling of the submaxillary glands, and frequently, also, of one or both the parotids. The tumefaction may develop rapidly, be accompanied by marked tenderness upon pressure, or hard and insensible to the touch; decline more or less speedily by resolution, or linger into a decided and exhaustive sequel, as a suppurating abscess. It is seldom that a case of malignant diphtheria runs through its whole course of development and decline without a prominent and important lesion of one or more of the cervical glands, a symptom which not unfrequently adds greatly to the increased labor of respiration, and to the possibility of a fatal issue.

The Larynx and Trachea.—That portion of the respiratory mucous membrane which lines these organs, is sometimes the seat of the diphtheritic deposit. The exudation may commence in the larynx or trachea, but is more prone to follow upon that which takes place in the throat and fauces. Sometimes the curtain which envelops the latter, extends through the glottis into the vocal organ, and encroaches upon the trachea, even down to its bifurcation. Such a case would be accompanied by extreme dyspnœa. Dr. Wade, an eminent English authority, says, however, that in no case which he has dissected, was the laryngeal exudation continuous with the faucial.

Sometimes the shreds of pseudo-membrane, of which I have spoken, embarass the voice and respiration by adhering to the lips of the glottis, and hanging down through its orifice into the larynx. In either case, the symptom is a bad one. Aphonia, with croupy respiration, will apprise you that the lesion has invaded the larynx. Symptoms of asphyxia may present themselves. The cough is ringing, whistling, metallic, croupy. Deglutition may have become less difficult, the faucial deposit and congestion succeeded by a more healthy appearance of the surface, and the swelling of the neighboring glands subsided, but the danger is greatly increased. The countenance becomes livid, as the respiration is more and more embarrassed.

The skin will be cold, the pulse feeble and declining in frequency, and death finally result, it may be by the most horrible and heart-rending strangulation, or without a sigh or a groan.

You will not fail to recognize that, where the larynx and trachea are invaded by the peculiar morbid deposit of diphtheria, which, indeed, occurs much less frequently than physicians are led to suppose, the case has virtually resolved itself, in so far at least as the local symptoms are concerned, into one of membranous croup. There is this qualification, however, to my last remark. In the diphtheritic croup—for under these circumstances the two affections are become one—the lesion is the result of constitutional causes, and is secondary upon other general and local symptoms. A certain substantive poison is present in the system, and has worked these successive changes. In the case of genuine membranous croup, the last-named pathological peculiarities are wanting.

The Nasal Symptoms.—In certain epidemics, the nares become a frequent seat of membranous deposit. M. Bretonnau cautions us that, in occasional instances, the disease begins at the nostrils, and extends thence in a most insidious manner. Usually, however, the nasal deposition occurs at a later period of the disease, and subsequent to the existence of the faucial symptoms already enumerated. When formed, there may be stringy shreds which hang out from the nostrils, or complete membranous casts of them visible at their outlet. These casts, or tubes, have an opaque, cartilaginous appearance, and are, in general, so regularly formed as to be quite characteristic. They appear thoroughly organized, and adhere quite firmly to the subjacent texture. Sometimes they are detached and dislodged by the acrid discharges from the nares, or by the concussion of the cough, or by a persistent picking of the nostrils by the little patient himself. This result, unless promptly healed by a re-organization of effused plasma, is apt to be followed by epistaxis, and on this account is not to be induced intentionally.

In certain very malignant cases, the pseudo-membrane is

not formed in the nares. The coryza, from the first, is too acrid and erosive. It disorganizes both the epithelial and the sub-mucous layers of the pituitary membrane, leaving the free surface raw and denuded. Or, it may be covered by a pasty, granular coating of feeble organization. In either case, the sanious ichor which filters away is septic in its very nature, and whether it be contained within the nasal cavities, or brought into contact with the lips and cheeks of the patient, will destroy the life of the tissues.

I have witnessed examples in which some weeks would elapse before the disorganizing effect of this poisonous matter upon the surface of the upper lip, and the immediate vicinity of the nostrils, would have entirely disappeared.

The nasal organ will, in many examples of the diphtheria maligna, be so occluded as to prevent the child from breathing freely, unless his mouth is kept open. He cannot lie down with comfort, if his head is not elevated by pillows. His respiration is loud and snoring, and will sometimes be so oppressed, after he has slept for a brief interval, as to cause him to waken suddenly out of sleep, start up in bed, and show signs of temporary delirium. This symptom is more marked in case the larger glands about the neck are so tumefied as to encroach upon, or block up the faucial cavity.

The Membranous Deposit in Various Localities.—From what has been already said, you will infer that the seat of the diphtheritic deposit will vary in different cases. In a table constructed by MM. Rilliet and Barthez, we find the relative frequency of membranous exudation, observed by them in various positions, to be as follows:

Upon the tonsils alone	6.
Upon the tonsils and some part of the soft palate	4.
Upon the tonsils, the velum palati, and the pharynx	6.
Upon the tonsils and pharynx	5.

The bronchial mucous membrane is sometimes the seat of the diphtheritic lesion. The deposit may take place in any of the larger bronchii, but seldom extends to the ultimate bronchial or capillary tubes. The symptoms indicative of this most serious complication would be a more or less embarrassed condition of respiration, a decided bronchial rhonchus, and a dry and unsatisfactory cough. After some hours, there would be great danger of pulmonary congestion and pneumonia. In some cases of the kind, the lungs have been found completely paralyzed from the rapid sealing up of the bronchial surfaces, so as suddenly to suspend the process of sanguification. As you will anticipate, the danger is increased in proportion as the disease interferes with this most vital function.

In less malignant cases, Prof. J. Y. Simpson is authority for the fact that this exudation may occur upon the free surface of the uterine mucous membrane ; and Prof. DeGraafe, in a recent issue of the *Archiv. für Ophthalmologie*, calls attention to a variety of ophthalmia which is characterized by its formation upon the conjunctiva and adjacent textures in the vicinity of the eye. M. Trousseau* devotes a clinical lecture to the consideration of palpebral, cutaneous, vulvular, vaginal, anal, prœputial and buccal diphtheria.

The Hæmorrhagic Symptoms.—From the breaking down of the crasis of the blood, the marked adynamia, and the more or less general disposition to the disorganization of the mucous structures, you would anticipate a liability to dangerous hæmorrhages. In all attacks of malignant diphtheria, hæmorrhages are apt to occur, and are not unfrequently intractable and quite uncontrollable by the best means at command. Of the different varieties, that from the nose is the more frequent. The reason is apparent. The capillary vessels are either left gaping open by the corrosive action of the pituitary mucus, or the blood is so thinned as to transude with the greatest facility. A passive flow may take place from the throat and fauces, from the separation of the exudation, leaving a denuded and vascular surface quite free to bleed, until a fresh supply of plasma has organized to cover it again. Any one of the free surfaces

* *Clinique Medicale*, Tome I., Page 343.

named as liable to become the seat of the diphtheritic deposit may suffer from a more or less troublesome hæmorrhage.

The most fatal symptom, however, is a form of purpura which sometimes occurs in the worst type of this disease. I have witnessed but one example of the kind, and, excepting only one other, have not read a detailed account of this fatal complication. This case is copied into Trousseau's clinical work, to which I have just referred,* from M. Peter's *Recherches sur la Diphthérite*, Paris, 1860. I have translated it for your benefit:

Case.—" August 1st, 1858, I was called from the Hospital des Enfants to 29 Rue de Sèvres to visit the young Marie P. This child had had a high fever for twenty-four hours, and for ten hours an intense sore throat. When I saw the patient, I recognized the tonsillitis, and noticed the commencement of an eruption resembling that of scarlatina. The fourth day of the disease the fever increased, the patient coughed, and I diagnosed the existence of a pneumonia upon the right side, an unusual complication of scarlatina. * * * * * The next day, August 5th, a thin, inflammatory coating was developed upon each of the amygdalæ; the fever was intense, the scarlatinous eruption had a violet tint; the general condition presented all the symptoms of adynamia. * * * * * * *

" 7th. The blister, (which had been applied over the right chest), had ulcerated and its surface was covered with an exudation. The false membranes had increased in thickness, and extended from the tonsils to the veil of the palate; were grayish in color and emitted a fœtid odor. * * * * * * * *

" 8th. The nose commenced to run, and at the orifice of the left nostril, I discovered a rudiment of false membrane. The scarlatinous eruption was a little less violet, but the fever remained high. The blister, ulcerated upon its borders, spread itself at the same time that the exudation which covered it was thickened. Meanwhile, far from resolving itself, the pneumonia increased in extent; there was a murmur with bronchophony in the inferior half of the right lung.

" From the 9th to the 11th the general condition grew still worse. Here and there thin shreds of epidermis were detached

* Vol. I., page 341.

from the arms, the thighs, and the eruption had faded somewhat; but the fever remained violent, and the patient exhaled from the mouth and the nose a fœtid odor. The alæ nasi were excoriated. From these orifices there flowed an acrid liquid which also excoriated the superior lip, and one could discover an exudation which curtained the interior of the nasal fossæ. The posterior throat was invaded by the pseudo-membranous deposit, and deglutition had become very difficult. Despite frequent injections into the nostrils and throat, the odor remained as before.

"On the 12th I found evidences of a commencing pneumonia in the left lung; while in the right one I heard rales which were almost gurgling; and there was an abundant expectoration of purulent and fœtid matter. An eruption resembling that of the scarlet-fever reappeared; the excoriations of the superior lip were covered with diphtheritic exudations. Upon the neck I saw two bullæ of pemphigus.

"13th. The excoriated bullæ were already coated with the exudation; numerous petechiæ, some scorbutic ecchymosis, appeared upon points where pressure had been exercised; there was an hæmorrhage from the blistered surface, and epistaxis; the false membranes upon the posterior wall of the throat (pharynx) were inflated with blood.

"14th. Bloody expectoration indicated to me the existence of a pulmonary hæmorrhage; there was hæmaturia, and enterorrhagiæ, accidents which I had foreseen, and which, I had the day previous announced to the family. The same day, and as I expected it also, the voice was changed, became hoarse, the false membranes having invaded the larynx. In the evening the voice was still more decidedly croupal.

"The night was the most anxious, and the patient died in early morning of the 15th of August, on the fifteenth day from the commencement of the disease."

LECTURE III.

Diphtheria Maligna Continued.—*The disorders of the Alimentary Function.—Ditto of the Urinary Function.—Albuminuria.—Uræmia.—Deranged Innervation.—Paralytic Symptoms and Sequelæ.*—Differential Diagnosis.—*From the Croup.—Case.—From Scarlatina Maligina.—From Gangrenous Pharyngitis*—Prognosis—*The Fever as a criterion of the severity of the attack.—Untoward Cerebral Symptoms.—Complicated with Uræmia.—Abscesses of tonsils and cervical glands.—Danger of Nasal Diphtheria.—Translation to the Larynx and Trachea.—Case.—Hæmorrhage from Mucous surfaces an unfavorable symptom.—Danger not always proportioned to the extent of pseudo-membranous deposit.—Paralytic symptoms not necessarily unfavorable.—Lingering convalescence deceptive.—Significance of Epidemic peculiarities and types.*

Gentlemen:—

I propose, in this Lecture, to continue the analysis of the more prominent symptoms of the Diphtheria Maligna, its diagnosis, and its prognosis. We shall first direct your attention to the

Disorders of the Alimentary Function.—Under the head of Febrile Symptoms, I have already spoken of a loss of appetite as an early feature of the diphtheria maligna. There are two causes upon which this symptom may depend:

1. The swelling and inflammation of the throat and fauces,

which interferes mechanically with deglutition, and occasions such suffering as to destroy any remaining desire for food.

2. An unnatural condition of the alimentary mucous membrane, which deranges the complex function of digestion, and destroys the local sensations which afford the foundation of a healthy appetite.

Where the throat symptoms do not appear in the early stage of the complaint, the appetite is not always lost, but may continue good. Now and then the patient will eat heartily whenever food is proffered, or indeed, demand it for himself. Usually, however, one or the other of the causes named, or it may be both combined, serve not alone to destroy the desire for a nourishing aliment, but also to excite a disgust or loathing of it in any form whatever.

Beside the anorexia, cases of diphtheria maligna are frequently characterized by gastric suffering and distress which differ in degree only from that to which your attention has been called when speaking of the diptheria simplex. As large a proportion as four-fifths of the examples of this form of the disease which have fallen under my personal notice, have presented this symptom. The pain in the epigastrium is usually dull and weighty in character, not acute and intermittent, but steady and constant, resembling that which dyspeptics sometimes experience at a given time after their meals. By-and-by the region of the stomach becomes sensitive to pressure, and vomiting or diarrhœa may result. If cold water be swallowed it increases the gastric uneasiness and distress.

As a rule, vomiting is not so frequent a precursor of the diphtheritic lesion as it is of the appearance of the exanthem in the eruptive fevers. It is more liable to come on after the throat symptoms are well developed, and the unnatural secretions of the fauces are thrust into the stomach, through the canal of the pharynx and the æsophagus. These secretions are tough, acrid, and indigestible, and, like those common to infantile pneumonia, are swallowed into that viscus for the simple reason that one cannot teach the little patient how to expectorate them. If not vomited, this matter may pass into the intestines, and ultimately prove an irritating source of unnatural discharges from this tract, in the form of stool.

Dr. Ormerod* remarks, that, "One of the most troublesome symptoms is vomiting—a symptom only to be subdued by promptly substituting nutritive enemata for nourishment taken by the mouth. This irritability of stomach may arise, in some measure, from the putrilage which is constantly trickling down the throat, and in an atmosphere upon whose effluvia the poor sufferer may be said to live. But there is a further cause than this; for the vomiting will continue sometimes after the diseased surfaces have assumed the appearance of a healthy sore, if they have not actually healed. It is not merely a troublesome, but a very dangerous symptom, through which many patients die, and it is never to be looked upon without great anxiety as to the result of the cases in which it occurs."

In some instances, or rather in certain epidemics, the diarrhœa is the first symptom complained of. The stools will be frequent, copious, liquid, offensive in odor, and of an orange color. They may be painless, and, in some cases, quite involuntary. Generally, however, their passage is accompanied by a considerable degree of suffering, and sometimes with marked tenesmus. In a few instances, I have known the diarrhœa to be characterized by as many as three or four stools, passed in rapid succession, the paroxysm being repeated as often as twice or thrice in twenty-four hours, and followed by a complete intermission of the symptom. As the more malignant attack progresses, the stools change in consistency, color, etc. They become thicker, of a dark-brown or blackish cast, and, in the worst cases, are found to contain shreds of the diphtheritic false membrane analagous to that usually found in the throat. The dark color of the dejections is due to the passage of the exudation through the primæ viæ; and the shreds of false membrane are the exfoliations of the diphtheritic deposit from some portion of the alimentary mucous surface. A troublesome tenesmus will sometimes result from the location of the deposit in the large intestine where, through reflex action, it becomes a source of constant inclination to stool.

*London Lancet, March 1862, page 166.

During the prevalence of diphtheria it is not unusual for the physician to be called upon to treat a greatly increased number of patients among both adults and children who are suffering with some lesion of the intestinal mucous membrane. This leison may be functional or organic, will be accompanied by fever of a remittent type, indigestion, and vomiting or diarrhœa. At this moment, in mid-winter, there are few families in this city a majority of whose members are not thus afflicted. Young infants seem especially liable to attacks of an intractable diarrhœa, from which, at this season, they are usually exempted. This feature of the epidemic is so remarkable as to call to mind the essay of Dr. Kidd, presented to the British Homœopathic Society in 1858, in which he argues a striking analogy in the etiology and progress of diphtheria and cholera. I am satisfied that, in the present epidemic of the diphtheria in the city of Chicago, all that is wanting to render bowel complaints equally prevalent and troublesome as in cholera seasons, is that the mind and imagination of the laity be directed to the subject.

Disorders of the Urinary Function.—The sudden accession of the fever, in an attack of diphtheria maligna, frequently arrests the secretion and discharge of urine. Upon inquiry, you may learn that the patient, who has been ill for twenty-four or thirty-six hours before you were called to visit him, has voided little of none of this fluid. The cessation of its flow may be due to one of two causes. Either its secretion by the kidneys is entirely suppressed, or influences affecting the nervous sympathies of the bladder may have caused it to be retained in that viscus. If its elements have not been drained away from the blood, as in its healthy elimination, you are aware that fatal consequences will impend to the nervous centres, as the brain and spinal cord. A total suppression in the excretion of urea may, and frequently does, give rise to cramps and convulsions, especially in the later stages of the diphtheria maligna. Or, if not sufficiently injurious to occasion such manifest disorder, it may increase the danger by affording an additional source of blood-poisoning.

The retention of the urine in the bladder indicates a derangement of the nervous filaments supplied to that organ. The chain of reflex sympathies is broken. Volition, if directed to the relief of the disability, has no power to remedy it. The sphincter vesicæ are paralyzed, and this symptom of retention of urine in the bladder is another evidence that the diphtheritic poison has a powerful affinity for the nervous system, and spends its first force upon the centres of animal and organic life.

Either or both these symptoms may soon yield, and a free flow of urine be established. Or, the amount secreted will be lessened, and its quality much changed. If the fever has been violent, and the alimentary disorder is marked in degree, it will be high-colored, scanty, offensive, and voided with more or less of suffering and tenesmus. Stranguary is, in my experience more frequent among adults than among children. The increased color of the urine will be due to the presence of an undue proportion of biliary substances, particularly of the biliverdin, or coloring matter of the bile.

But the most important symptom indicative of urinary derangement in diphtheria is albuminuria. Dr. Wade, of Birmingham, England,* was the first to call the attention of the profession to this complication. I shall base a few remarks upon his extensive and well-digested observations on this subject.†

Albumen may sometimes be detected in the urine of patients suffering with the diphtheria maligna at a very early period of the disease, while again, it is not found to be present until about the seventh or eighth day. At this time, when the disorder has a natural tendency to terminate, there appears an increased liability to albuminuria, as it is technically termed. The exudation in the throat, if not interfered with, in a majority of cases, is ready to drop off and leave the surface beneath in a tolerably healthy state, at about this period. The fever has declined, or perhaps, disappeared entirely. At once the little

*Observations on Diphtheria, by W. F. Wade, B. A. &c. &c., 1858.

†London Lancet, for November, 1862, page 267.

patient is become worse, there appears to have been a relapse. The parents think that he has "taken cold," they know not in what manner. There will be one, or it may be more febrile paroxysms, and the child which was so decidedly convalescent is ill again. By means of appropriate tests we discover that the milky hue of the urine is due to the presence of albumen in it. The kidneys afford a species of discharge which may or may not be regarded as critical.

Dr. Wade thinks that albuminuria in diphtheria is not necessarily attended by any obvious symptoms of an unfavorable character. Where, however, it is to be regarded as an evidence of organic degeneration of the kidneys, it becomes a more grave and significant symptom. Indications of this kind are found in a "dimunition in the quantity of urine excreted; suppression of the lithates; nervous symptoms—as indifference to surrounding objects, somnolence, coma,—coincidently with the commencement of the albuminuria, and not referable to any other known cause but the kidney complication."

Greenhow is of opinion that the albuminuria of diphtheria, will in most cases be observable at an earlier period of the disease than when it occurs in scarlatina. He, indeed, offers this as a diagnostic symptom separating the pathology of the two affections.

On the contrary, Dr. Wade "has not observed the early presence of albumen in the urine, which, from the concurrent testimony of trustworthy observers, no doubt frequently occurs." He offers two explanations of this fact, viz: that "most of his cases have been seen in consultation, after fatal symptoms have supervened," and that his "plan of treatment has long been directed to the prevention of the kidney complication."

In my lectures upon the physiology and pathology of the uropoietic organs your attention was especially directed to the etiology, diagnosis, prognosis, and treatment of albuminuria. You are aware that the presence of albumen in the urine, like that of blood in the sputa of a patient ill with pneumonia, is to be regarded merely as a symptom. As such it will vary in its significance with the different circumstances in which it is found. It may constitute a marked symptom of Bright's degeneration of the kidneys, of vesical catarrh, or pyelitis, diseases of the prostrate gland, gonorrhoea, or of ordinary urethretis. You will of necessity find albumen present in the urine voided by patients having hæmaturia.

In the diphtheria, however, as in certain varieties of eclampsia, hysteria, and some other affections, this is a marked feature of the disease. The urine will appear more or less cloudy, and the application of heat, or of one of the mineral acids, or even of corrosive sublimate in solution, will cause a more or less dense precipitation of albumen.

Uræmia, arising from an imperfect elimination of certain organic elements of the urine from the blood, may or may not be attended by albuminuria. But this latter symptom is seldom present in diphtheritic cases, without more or less of the former. Every example of albuminuria accompanying or supervening upon the diphtheria maligna, is liable to be characterized, at some portion of its course, by certain nervous symptoms, which vary in intensity in proportion with the suppression of the excretory function of the kidneys.

Urea, like opium, has a strong tendency to act upon the brain. Dr. Alonzo Clark* says: "Its vital affinites are for the cerebral matter."

If the glandular epithelium lining the tubes of Ferrein and of Bellini, is decayed, broken up into a fine granular matter, exfoliated, diseased, or functionally deranged, the nervous centres will be poisoned by the vitiated blood which is brought to them. Here is an internal source of zymotic disorder. While, therefore, there may be symptoms of uræmia, unattended by albuminuria, you are not to forget that the presence of albumen in the urine of a diphtheritic patient, implies an impending danger from a retention in the blood of certain elements which should be depurated from it.

This leads me to speak of diphtheritic albuminuria as critical in its nature. When we reflect that the epithelial mucous

* Bulletin of N. Y. Academy of Medicine, vol. 1, p. 472.

surfaces suffer most severely from the structural lesions characteristic of the diphtheria, and that the allied functions of diaphoresis and of diuresis are prone to derangement throughout the whole course of the disease, it is not strange that the delicate coating of the basement membrane lining the uriniferous tubes is so often the seat of some pathological lesion. If to this we add that a chief characteristic of the diphtheria appears to consist in a more or less excessive and præternatural waste of albumen from the blood-plasma, either by means of the spendthrift process of exudation and organization of false membrane, upon mucous or abraded surfaces, of abscesses which discharge it most lavishly, or of intestinal or cutaneous excreta which sap the vital resources, we see an additional reason why, in the very nature of things, a critical albuminuria must sometimes result.

Whether your individual experience will confirm this view, I am unable to say. One thing, however, is true, that within the range of my own observation, and that of my more immediate and reliable professional friends, albuminuria has not been present in any marked degree in those cases which have been characterized by the free formation and discharge of pus, or of a pale-colored serum from abscesses, by a very extensive deposit of the pseudo-membrane upon the respiratory or alimentary mucous surfaces, by exhausting sweats, or by a copious and intractable diarrhœa.

The extravasation of the liquor sanguinis upon the aforenamed free surfaces, in such amount as not only to overburden the capacity of the intestinal lympathics to absorb it again, but to hazard the organic integrity of the tissues themselves, may be regarded as another evidence of the critical nature of the diphtheritic albuminuria. M. Andral long ago recorded his observation, that losses of albumen, through unnatural outlets, were characterized by a corresponding decrease of its relative proportion in the blood. This, at least, will explain an important source of the extreme prostration of system met with in diphtheria; although M. Trousseau,* does not endorse the

---

* Vide *Clinique Medicale*, Tome I., Page 369.

view that it may prove even an indirect source of the paralytic phenomena of diphtheria. It also explains a fact observed by Greenhow, that albuminuria "does not always coincide with great severity in the other symptoms."

The morphotic elements of the urine in this disease will vary in different cases. In some, the microscope will reveal more or less distinct casts of the uriniferous tubes. These casts will appear either in the form of cylinders, exfoliated from the tubes of Ferrein in the cortical portion of the kidney, or of grouped, nucleated cells, arranged in the form of a honeycomb, which are known to consist of detached portions of the epithelial lining of the tubules of Belleni in the medullary structure of that organ. You need not, however, always expect to find them even in the more malignant examples of the diphtheria. They are not, indeed, so constant an element of the urine in either form of this disease as in the desquamative stage of scarlatina, and erysipelas, or in puerperal eclampsia. Dr. Helmuth* says: "Casts of the tubuli uriniferi have been seen in the urine; but I have often known great albuminous deposit to be present, and not uriniferous casts." My own experience confirms this statement, which I find is also endorsed by Dr. D. F. Condie† in the following quotation: "The albuminous urine, even when most marked and profuse, would occasionally be found entirely free from tubal casts."

I have dwelt upon this symptom of the diphtheria, gentlemen, because it gives us a key to the pathology of the disease which the honest and earnest practitioner cannot afford to dispense with. We are told that therapeutical indications should be based upon the *totality* of the symptoms presented. If you shall attempt to treat the more aggravated form of diphtheria, regardless of the significance of albuminuria as one of its principal concomitants, your prescriptions will frequently prove unscientific and necessarily unsuccessful. Let it be your endeavor to attain such a broad and comprehensive view

---

*A Treatise on Diphtheria; its nature, pathology, etc., St. Louis, 1862, p. 70.

† Proceedings of Philadelphia County Medical Society for 1862.

of the nature of the disease in its very essence, as shall render its minutest details of the utmost therapeutical service.

Deranged Innervation.—Evidences of a disordered innervation are presented in diphtheria, in abnormal conditions of the circulation, of animal heat, of the motor and sensational functions, and in derangements of the special senses. The fever, marked by the extreme heat of the surface, which may indicate a temperature as high as 110° or 111° Fahrenheit, and the frequent, irritable pulse, derives its most prominent symptoms from an affection of the nervous centres of animal and organic life. Of these features of diphtheria we have already spoken.

The nerves of sensation and of motion are subject to various disorders of function in this disease. The most frequent of these is a species of paralysis, which is more or less marked and persistent. The sensory filaments distributed to the skin become less responsive to the action of irritants of one variety or another. This constitutes a species of anæsthesia, which may be local or general. Sometimes the sensibility of the surface of one arm, or of a side of the face, of the neck, the trunk, or the lower extremities, will be almost or quite obliterated. Or, it may tingle and prickle with unnatural sensations which are a source of great annoyance to those patients who are old enough to specify the nature of their sufferings. One patient told me that her skin felt as if thousands of little needles were piercing it, these unnatural sensations coming in paroxysms, and being almost insupportable.

Again, instead of a loss of responsiveness on the part of the sensory filaments of the surface, the delicacy of their function is increased. The skin is super-sensitive. The mother or nurse will call your attention to the fact that the little patient has been seized with a mortal dread of being touched. To make an attempt to move him, or to apply one's hand to his body, will almost set him into convulsions. I have seen children ill with the diphtheria maligna, whose sufferings in this regard were extreme. The necessary manipulations for feeding them, supplying them with drink, etc., would subject them to a species of torture which was as real as any other evidence of suffering experienced. Exposure to currents of cool air aggravates this symptom. After some time, if it continue, the patient becomes morbidly irritable and petulant. Nothing pleases him. But, because he is cross, you are not to conclude this a favorable symptom. Peevishness is sometimes indicative of a most dangerous hyperæsthesia of the nervous centres, forboding convulsions, and a fatal declension of the vital power.

The motor apparatus is also subject to derangement. Paralysis of some of the muscles is not an unfrequent accompaniment, or sequel, of severe attacks of diphtheria. This affection may involve the capacity of motion in one limb or all of them—may induce paraplegia or hæmiplegia. It may affect the delicate muscles of the eye, or of the throat and pharynx, of the circulatory vessels, or of the alimentary canal. The derangment in the supply of motor force to the part, may involve its entire or partial withdrawal. Sometimes, a series of irregular and involuntary contractions, resembling those of the voluntary muscles in Chorea St. Viti, are produced. These are more frequently clonic, seldom tonic in their nature. Where paralysis occurs, it does not usually obliterate the function of both sets of filaments. Sensation will generally remain where motility is lost, and *vice versa.* This is a significant circumstance, more especially when considered with reference to motor paralysis of some of the interior passages. If, for example, the little patient's brain were not advertised, through the afferent fibres, of the presence of a foreign body introduced into his throat, the muscular walls of which are paralyzed, there would be a constant liability to strangulation, a result which it is possible, artificially, to avert.

There is one peculiarity of diphtheritic paralysis, to which I should direct your attention. Whenever it is present, in any form, the bowels are apt to be constipated, notwithstanding the general epidemic may be characterized by a troublesome diarrhœa in the great majority of cases. The danger from the paralytic complications and sequelæ will be proportioned to the period of the disease, and the organ in which they occur, the physical strength of the patient, and the function which is implicated. If it occur very early in the attack, and be accompanied by evidences of extreme debility, its significance would be more serious. If it should involve the respiratory or circulatory muscles, the most serious consequences might result. In my next lecture, I shall direct your attention to the causes of this most peculiar and important symptom.

Differential Diagnosis.—What I have to say under this head will be devoted to those points of pathological difference which separate the diphtheria maligna from the croup, from scarlatina maglina, and from gangrenous pharyngitis.

From the Croup.—You are doubtless aware that distinguished authorities, among whom are Bretonneau, Trousseau, West, and others, believe these affections are identical. The general points of difference between the diphtheria maligna and pseudo-membranous croup, concern the mode and manner of attack, the symptoms of its more active stage, and the sequelæ.

Both diseases are, in a great majority of cases, idiopathic. But while the croup sets in abruptly, without angniose symptoms, as œdema of the tonsils, a partial obstruction of the guttural cavity, discoloration of the mucous membrane lining the throat and fauces, with difficulty of swallowing, or a burning heat of the skin and delirium, these are the very symptoms which mark the advent of an attack of diphtheria. Most authorities locate the commencement of the croupal lesion in the larynx and trachea. But Bretonneau, Guersant and Trousseau affirm that, in the generality of cases, it commences in the pharynx, and finally invades the vocal organ proper. It appears certain, however, that the mode of attack in the two diseases is different. A child having retired to rest in perfect health, will be seized with the croup in the middle of the night. You may examine the fauces and pharynx never so closely, but will find no evidence of capillary engorgement in the faucial or pharyngeal mucous membrane.

In the diphtheria, if the throat symptoms are present at all in its earlier stages, you will discover some evidence of a local inflammation. We do not look for a patch upon the tonsils as a characteristic of the membranous croup. Croup very rarely, almost never, commences with epigastric uneasiness, vomiting or diarrhœa. The converse of this is true of the diphtheria. There is not a symptom of the croup, which pertains to the manner of its coming, that does not lead one to regard it in the light of a local affection, which, from deranging the function of the very gateway to the respiratory system, may hazard the welfare of the organism in a secondary manner. The throat and faucial affection in diphtheria are, as it were, engrafted upon a proper constitutional disorder, the local unfolding of a general derangement.

Let me illustrate the fact, that, in many examples of the diphtheria, the larynx and trachea are only reached by the exudation after the disease has made considerable progress.

Case.—Lulu B., aged five and a-half years, a playmate of little Eva R., whose symptoms were narrated in my first lecture, and who, *en passant*, has convalesced with slight faucial paralysis, was seized with a violent fever, and an excruciating pain in the left tonsil and submaxillary region.

January 14th.—The fever caused her to be delirious, and the pain was so very acute that she could not tolerate the least motion. The swelling was inconsiderable. Internally, both tonsils were enlarged, and the left one shewed a patch of false membrane of the size of a dime. Deglutition not very difficult; skin hot and dry; urine free in amount, but highly colored. The next day, the left tonsil was covered, as with a cap of the diphtheritic deposit, and signs of the exudation were visible upon the right one. A thin but acrid saliva flowed from the mouth. Mind clear; is interested in objects around, the school children, etc. The third day, pain in the neck greatly relieved, but both tonsils are completely enveloped. Other symptoms the same. Ate a little plain custard, and drank some milk. The fourth day she coughed up the coating from the left tonsil, a specimen of which deposit I am prepared to show you in the field of the microscope at the close of the lecture. The exudation upon the right one is thinner, and shrivelled. No new deposit anywhere within sight. Patient seems convalescent. Family, and all interested, much encouraged. The fifth day, the little pet has a croupy cough, sibilant respiration, and her complexion has changed. Lips look purplish; expression anxious and imploring; throws herself about in bed; springs up suddenly, at intervals, in order to catch her breath. Is sleepy, comatose, indifferent; urine retained for twelve hours, and albuminous. Pulse weak and irritable. In the evening, respiration croupy and sawing. These symptoms increased, the exudation extending to the lungs, and she died, in a comatose state, from pulmonary congestion, on the night of the sixth day.

Again, attacks of croup, in those who are predisposed thereto, may result at any time from wet feet, a sudden suppression of the sensible perspiration, or so slight a cause as sitting for a brief interval in a current of cool air. These trivial contingencies, which cluster about the era of childhood, seem never to be sufficient to produce an attack of genuine diphtheria. A specific cause is requisite for this purpose. It must enter the circulation as a specific nidus, which is afterwards to develope its own legitimate fruits. For this latter reason, the diphtheria prevails as an epidemic, while the croup does not. We say of a child, that he is congenitally predisposed to the croup; but we cannot know, beforehand, whether he is or is not susceptible to the action of the specific invisible diphtheritic cause. When the weather is damp and foggy, as in this city at the present time, cases of catarrhal croup occur so frequently as to call a physician from his bed, it may be, each night in the week. These cases are not to be mistaken for diphtheria.

The pseudo-membranous form of croup, is a much more rare and dangerous variety of the disease. But, I apprehend, the diagnosis between this and the diphtheria is equally distinct. In the first place, it is so seldom witnessed, that some physicians of enlarged experience have not been called upon to treat more than a very few examples of it. It is a local affection, which is confined to the larynx and trachea—is not infectious, neither malignant in its nature, and varies in its more characteristic symptoms and sequelæ from diphtheria.

The dyspnœa in croup is paroxysmal, and invariably worse at night. There is a true spasm of the laryngeal and tracheal muscular fibres. At intervals, the patient breathes almost naturally. In a few moments, especially if permitted to sleep, he is in a fit of suffocation again, which, by-and-by, alternates with relative repose. The ease and freedom of the respiratory movements in diphtheria, vary considerably at intervals; but these intervals occur irregularly during the day, as well as at night, and the relief afforded by them is less marked than in the case of croup.

There is no eruption in croup—no acrid coryza, no especial liability to hæmorrhages from the mucous membranes, no purpura, no alimentary disorder, and, excepting in very rare cases, no albuminuria. The glands about the neck are not swollen, and paralytic sequelæ are almost unknown as a result of this disease.

The true croup has never been communicated by inoculation upon mucous or abraded surfaces, as has the diphtheria. No one speaks of croupal deposits in the right side of the heart, upon the alimentary or uterine mucous membrane, or upon the surface of ulcerated or wounded cutaneous integument. Such peculiarities of the diphtheritic deposition are by no means rare.

I have said the croup was never epidemic. This remark needs qualification. There is a form of this disease which sometimes prevails, and with alarming fatality, in certain neighborhoods. There seems but little doubt that examples of this kind consist, essentially, of a complication of diphtheria and croup. The diphtheritic exudation, contrary to its more usual course, appears first upon the lining membrane of the larynx and trachea. All the more violent characteristics of malignant diphtheria, excepting only the lesion in the throat proper, are present. The exudation occurs, and its organization into a pseudo-membrane is effected upon a surface in which it at once occasions croupal symptoms. Diphtheritic concretions may be present upon the lips of the glottis, producing more or less of asphyxia. The timbre or tone of the voice is altered. The sound produced with each inspiratory effort is crowing and croupy. The remaining symptoms, and the final result, in a great majority of cases, assure us that these two terrible diseases may be united in a single patient. A prevalent pseudo-membranous croup is to be regarded, therefore, as having derived its epidemic qualities from an admixture with the diphtheria, while its nature and consequences are more threatening than when it occurs in sporadic cases. Excepting in this complicated form, nine-tenths of the cases of croup recover under appropriate treatment. This cannot be truly reported of the malignant diphtheria.

Dr. Helmuth records an important distinction between these two diseases: "In croup, we believe the membrane to be distinctly fibrinous, while in diphtheria it is albuminous in its character." Croup is inflammatory, while diphtheria is asthenic in character.

In my own professional experience, a predisposition to the croup does not appear to have increased the liability to attacks of the diphtheria. On the contrary, I have yet to see the first well-marked case of genuine uncomplicated diphtheria occurring in a croupy subject. Such little patients will sometimes fall victims to a combination of the two disorders, but it would appear that a proneness to croupy affections of the respiratory channels, affords a kind of exemption from diphtheritic disorders of the mucous membranes lining those parts which are subservient to deglutition.

Among adults, well authenticated cases of membranous croup are extremely rare. The converse of this is true of diphtheria, for adults are frequently seized, and sometimes die with it.

Dr. Hauner,* of the Children's Hospital, in Munich, draws

* *Journal fur Kinderkrankheiten.*

the following conclusions upon the differential diagnosis of croup from diphtheria:

"1. True laryngeal croup is a disease proper to childhood, and its cause is chiefly to be sought in the organization (the period of development) of the larynx at this period of life.

"2. The anatomy and physiology of the larynx sufficiently explain the nature of croup.

"3. It cannot be shown that croup is connected with any peculiarity of the blood crasis.

"4. True croup always commences in the larynx, and often passes downward into the trachea, etc., but it never passes upwards.

"5. Laryngeal croup is characterized by a pseudo-membrane of more or less extent.

"6. Laryngeal croup is to be carefully distinguished from diphtheritic croup, the latter always depending upon a peculiar blood crasis, as seen in other organs of enfeebled individuals.

"7. Diphtheritic croup is almost always secondary, and is not essentially different from croup in and after the acute exanthemata.

"8. The diphtheritic form begins, as a general rule, in the fauces, uvula, tonsils, etc., and extends hence downwards. It is very rare for it to commence in the larynx or trachea."

From Scarlatina Maligna.—This is the only form of scarlet fever with which the diphtheria maligna is likely to be confounded.

Prominent among the differential characteristics, is the type of the fever. In scarlatina it may be continuous throughout the whole course of the disease, notwithstanding the rash has appeared upon the surface. The heat of skin is persistent. In diphtheria, the febrile type is most frequently remittent, the heat of skin declines, and may even disappear during the remission. In scarlatina, the type of the fever is very apt to change from a continued to a remittent form, upon the appearance of the eruption. In diphtheria, it will not vary essentially from the commencement to the termination of the disease, no matter when the rash appears, or if it never appear. These febrile symptoms render the diphtheria more insidious in its approach than is the scarlet fever. In the one case, the subsidence of the paroxysm is very deceptive; in the other, the intensity and persistence of the fever are positively alarming.

The symptoms already specified as affording the chief diagnostic points between scarlatina and diphtheria simplex, are substantially the same for the diagnosis of this form of the disease from the scarlatina maligna. The angina, in scarlatina, has a specific determination to the faucial cavity. It does not invade the respiratory mucous surfaces—never degenerates into a species of croup, by a change of locality, as the diphtheritic exudation not unfrequently does.

The different color of the eruption; its rubeoloid eruption is less generally diffused than that of scarlatina; and the fact observed by Valleix, that desquamation of the cuticle occurs in the scarlatina, but not in the rash of diphtheria, are points to be considered in forming your diagnosis in a given case.

Scarlatina rarely commences with acute pains resembling rheumatism in the glands and muscles about the throat, or with severe otalgia. The opposite is true of diphtheria.

Scarlatina is much less liable than the diphtheria to be accompanied in its course, or followed by, symptoms indicative of disordered innervation. Cases of paralysis do, however, sometimes succeed scarlet fever, but it has been remarked that these are almost invariably fatal, while the opposite is true of the diphtheritic paralysis.

Dr. H. C. Preston* has never seen or heard of a tendency to anasarca, or other dropsical affection, occurring as a sequel to diphtheria, notwithstanding it so frequently follows scarlatina. This same distinction is recognized by West† and other distinguished authorities.

Dr. Condie says that, "Unlike what occurs in scarlatina, albumen has very seldom been detected in the urine during convalescence from diphtheria; never, unless it had been previously present."

Another diagnostic point, and one which might, perhaps, be considered sufficient to establish a wide and essential differ-

---

* U. S. Journal of Homœopathy, vol. 1, p. 239.

† Lectures on Diseases of Children, 1860, p. 326.

ence between these two diseases, is found in the fact that an attack of diphtheria is not a protective from scarlatina, and *vicê versa.*

And yet another is mentioned by Dr. Ormerod, that the exposure of lying-in women to the contagion of diphtheria, does not produce any ill consequences; while the same exposure to that of scarlatina is sufficient to induce almost certain death from puerperal fever.

Dr. Wm. Jenner, in a clinical lecture on diphtheria, its symptoms and treatment, says: "Diphtheria has been supposed to be modified scarlet fever, but the fact that it attacks indiscriminately those who have and those who have not had this disease, proves that it is altogether a different, though it may still be a closely-allied disease."

Both affections, however, frequently prevail in the same locality at the same time; and different members of the same family may experience either the one or the other, one having diphtheria, another scarlatina, and perhaps a third an admixture of both. In some cases, indeed, it would almost seem as if they were convertible, the one into the other. For this reason, certain eminent authorities believe them to be identical. This question is so well put by Dr. Wade,* that I copy *verbatim :*

"To those who find less difficulty in coming to a positive conclusion upon the point, I beg to recommend the following considerations:

(*a.*) "Scarlatina and diphtheria may be associated.

(*b.*) "Scarlatina is not necessarily accompanied by efflorescence, or by noticeable fever.

(*c.*) "Diphtheria may probably affect the system, without producing any throat exudation.

(*d.*) "Scarlatina may recur.

(*e.*) "Certain forms of scarlatina may be *accompanied* by albuminuria.

(*f.*) "Scarlatinal albuminuria does not necessarily produce dropsy; dropsy, in fact, is the exception in albuminuria *accompanying* scarlatina.

---

* London Lancet for November, 1862, p. 268.

(*g.*) "Any occasional form of a specific fever may become the type of an epidemic.

(*h.*) "Granting that scarlet fever and diphtheria are both zymotic disorders, we do not know what is the nature of their respective poisons."

It sometimes happens that diphtheria is secondary to scarlet-fever. Such complications are always of a serious character. Trousseau speaks of such cases as follows:

"They have an attack of scarlatina of medium severity; a little nightly delirium with scarcely any nervous complications; the pulse is tolerably frequent; the pain in the throat moderately severe. About the eighth or ninth day it seems that recovery is certain; the fever has fallen, the eruption disappeared, and we congratulate those who are most interested. At once a considerable swelling appears at the angle of the jaws; occupying not only this region, but extending to the neck, and sometimes to a part of the face; a santous, fœtid, abundant fluid flows from the nasal cavities; the tonsils are tumefied, the breath is insufferably offensive; the pulse is small and suddenly resumes its characteristic frequency; delirium and other nervous symptoms are reproduced; the delirium persists, coma supervenes, while the skin becomes cold, the pulse more and more feeble, and the patient dies gradually after three or four days, or it may be without warning, as by syncope."

From Gangrenous Pharyngitis.—The septic nature of the ulceration, which tends to a rapid sloughing of the soft parts beneath the epithelium; the lack of the filmy, pearly-looking, organized deposit upon the surface of the ulcers; the local hæmorrhage, and the odor, present a list of symptoms which are, in general, quite sufficient to distinguish the gangrenous pharyngitis from diphtheria. Add to these, that in this form of pharyngitis, there is little or no fever, no swelling of the tonsils, neither of the lymphatic glands, no eruption, no liability to translation of the lesion from the alimentary to the respiratory tract, no characteristic nervous symptoms or sequelæ, neither any especial implication of the urinary function, and their differential diagnosis is complete.

PROGNOSIS.—In the diphtheria maligna, the result will depend upon the gravity of the single and aggregate symptoms already enumerated.

If the fever is of a decidedly adynamic type, from the first invasion of the disease, with a dry, crisp, and brownish coated tongue, or this organ is red and pointed, smooth and glistening, as in certain cases of malignant scarlatina, or raw, like a piece of beef, the prognosis will be unfavorable. The same is true if the extreme heat and dryness of the skin, or the frequency and irritability of the pulse continue unabated. The chances for recovery would be lessened should the fever degenerate into a species of versatile typhus, and the patient become excessively loquacious, nervous or hysterical, during the whole day and night, disposed to jump up and run away, to take the cars, to go home, or to accomplish many other impossibilities. On the contrary, if the febrile paroxysm is become less marked and decided, with a slower, fuller, and more regular beat of the pulse, less heat of skin, a slight and grateful diaphoresis, and a moderation of the cerebral disturbance, there may yet remain some slight hope of recovery.

Untoward cerebral symptoms will be recognized in a preternatural activity of the brain and the intellectual faculties, impaired vision, amblyopia, muscæ volitantes, amaurosis, or in sluggishness of memory, confused ideas, sopor, and in manifestations of disturbance of function in the sensorial or motorial systems, as, for example, paralysis or convulsions. The significance of these symptoms will be in ratio with those indicative of serious disorder in the depurating process performed by the kidneys. In most cases of diphtheria, they do not appear, excepting in an advanced stage of the disease. I have already remarked that few cases of diphtheria are characterized, in their early stage, by convulsions; and paralysis, also, with the remaining nervous symptoms, is more frequently seen at a later period. The same is true of the urinary complication. Indeed, the period of greatest apprehension of danger from cerebral complication in diphtheria, appears to be that which corresponds with the advent of the albuminuria. This seems especially true of those examples in which the urine is not only loaded with albumen, but also contains numerous exfoliated tubal casts, signifying a structural lesion, which indicates the retention of certain post-organic, urinary matters in the blood. Trousseau to the contrary, notwithstanding, there is every reason to believe that uræmia, or the poisoning of the blood by this cause, is a chief source of the most serious consequences to the animal and organic nervous systems in malignant diphtheria.

One thing, at least, appears certain, that while simple albuminuria is not necessarily a fatal complication of the diphtheria, the presence in the urine of microscopical tubes, and other more obvious symptoms of renal derangement in regard of the eliminating process, are very apt to be accompanied by cerebral and nervous disorders, which, when added to the former, will necessitate an unfavorable prognosis. The little patient might possibly survive either the one or the other; but, when taken together, they are quite too formidable. The blood is doubly depraved by the addition of an internal visceral source of its corruption, and a more powerful blow is thus aimed at the integrity of the organic processes through the nervous system.

When the glands about the neck are greatly swollen, hard, and suppuration or resolution is retarded, cerebral congestion may result from a mechanical obstruction to the flow of the blood to and from the head. This condition of the brain is also unfavorable.

Abscesses of the tonsils, parotids, and other glands in the vicinity of the neck, may prove dangerous by occluding the superior air-passage, as well as by obstructing a free circulation in the cervical and cerebral vessels. It is always a bad sign if the process of suppuration in these abscesses is found to be very tardy and slow. If the adventitious membrane covering the tonsils and fauces, or any portion thereof, shall form again, after it has exfoliated, and the new coating shall be found to be more thoroughly organized, thicker and stronger than before, it is an evidence that the cure is not progressing favorably. If the faucial mucous membrane has an erysipelatous appearance, which, dating from the commencement of the attack, seems disposed to spread to adjacent parts, the gravity of the symptom should be recognized. An extensive sloughing of the substance of the tonsils, or of the oral or pharyngeal mucous membrane, indicates a depraved vitality in those parts which we may find it impossible to remedy.

But, in most instances, the danger from the throat symptoms, in this form of diphtheria, seems proportioned to the ease and freedom with which the lesion finally invades the neighboring parts. Nasal diphtheria may precede or follow the inflammation and exudation in the throat and fauces. In either case, it is an alarming symptom. Where it sets in at a late period in the course of the disease, it indicates a disposition on the part of the disorganizing process in the epithelium to spread to the respiratory mucous surfaces. In my own experience, it has been remarked that such an extension of the disease has almost invariably been followed by a deposit in the larynx, and manifest croupal symptoms. Indeed, wherever the acrid, diphtheritic coryza is found, there appears to be an extreme liability to this fearful complication, and I must, therefore, repeat my warning, that your prognosis in a case of this kind, shall be guarded, and your professional attentions most faithfully given. Here is a case in point:

Case.—Only yesterday, Jan. 23d, 1863, I was called at 9 A. M. to No. —, Fourth Avenue, to visit little Anna Porter H—, 13 months old. The little pet was apparently as well as usual, bright, cheerful, happy, and showed no other symptom of disease except the irritated nostril of which I have spoken. The nasal mucus had not excoriated the cheek, for it was small in amount, and not very acrid; but the pituitary membrane appeared somewhat raw and denuded, and the nostrils were larger and more patulous than is natural for a child of that age. She had a cough, as in ordinary influenza; her throat was not swollen, neither could I declare it congested and sore. She had a slight but not troublesome diarrhœa. In brief, the symptoms had been mistaken for influenza, which they most nearly resembled.

At 4 P. M., croupy symptoms were noticed. These increased as night came on, and I found her, at 1 in the morning, struggling for breath, and showing all the signs of extensive membranous deposit in the larynx and trachea. Toward daybreak she grew better, breathed more freely, the shrill, croupal sound of the cough and respiration gave place to a decided mucous râle, and I entertained hopes of her recovery.

At my next visit, at 8.30 A. M., the dyspnœa was most marked, she breathed rapidly, with a harsh, sawing sound, and the pulse was almost imperceptible. She did not recognize me. The face and lips were discolored, and I pronounced her to be dying from occlusion of the respiratory channels, by deposit of false membrane in them. There was every symptom of pulmonary congestion due to this cause. She died at half past two, half an hour previous to this lecture, and but little more than twenty-four hours after I had first prescribed for the *apparently* trivial symptoms afore-named.

The occurrence of epistaxis in one who is subject to it may not always be looked upon as an unfavorable symptom. Where, however, it happens in the person of a patient who has seldom or never experienced it before, and is evidently due to the extremely acrid nature of the nasal flow, or to a thin and impoverished condition of the blood, its appearance may lead you to anticipate a like dangerous accident from other mucous surfaces, and in very malignant cases, a deposit beneath the epidermis in the form of purpura hæmorrhagica. If a simple nose-bleed in the later stages of the attack of diphtheria do not yield promptly to ordinary remedies, you should recognize that the crasis of the blood is dissolved, and that, possibly, you may not be able to arrest it entirely, and consequently fail to cure the case.

The danger, in a case of malignant diptheria, is not proportioned to the amount or extent of the exudation, providing it does not encroach upon some portion of the respiratory tract. The membrane may be thick and strong, sufficient in extent to curtain the whole faucial and superior pharyngeal cavity, and yet the case ultimately terminate in recovery. If it is confined to this locality, and does not invade the larynx and trachea, or the nasal mucous surface; if it is not so septic as to hazard the growth and repair of the submucous structures, the patient may do well. It is a favorable sign to witness the deposit growing thinner and more transparent or shrivelled and contracted, from day to day, and finally drop off spontaneously without a new one forming in its stead. But you are not to forget that this precise period may be the one of greatest danger from the formation of new membranes upon more vital parts, and especially within and below the glottis. You remember the case of little Lulu B—; that she did finely until at the very time when the coating from the left tonsil had been detached and expectorated, and that which enveloped the right one promised the same change within the next twenty-four hours, croupy symptoms, with albuminuria, and partial coma were developed, and her death was the rapid and unavoidable result.

I have already said that the albuminuria may be regarded as a serious symptom of the diphtheria, when it furnishes the evidence of such a degree of structural and functional lesion of the kidneys as will occasion uræmic poisoning. In other words, if you have reason to believe that any considerable share of the nervous symptoms present are due to an incomplete depuration of the blood by these organs, your prognosis must be qualified, if indeed it is not always unfavorable.

If the paralytic disorder is located in the extremities and less vital parts, it is not to be regarded as a very serious symptom or sequel of this disease. If, however, it is found to affect the thoracic or abdominal viscera the consequences are more to be dreaded. There appears to be a strong disposition, in most cases of diphtheria, to react favorably against the various disorders of innervation, if we except only the great and sudden prostration which so frequently and almost invariably results. Indifference to surrounding objects, sterterous breathing, coma, and convulsions, are symptoms which portend evil consequences to the general organism.

There are yet other details which should lead you carefully to qualify your prognosis. "In many diseases, it is a favorable sign if the patients are no worse from day to day, for in such cases we only want to gain time for the storm to blow over, and all will be well; but it is not so in diphtheria. If our patient is not better from day to day, as the disease draws near the end of the second week, we have every reason, from the circumstance, for thinking him worse. The chances of delay are altogether against him. Drowsiness is not the 'saving sleep' of returning health, and a sudden diminution of the frequency of the pulse, (I have seen it suddenly sink to 28 in the minute,) is commonly a symptom of failure of the action of the heart. Unless all the symptoms concur in assuring us that our patient is doing well, we must distrust the quiet sleep and the slackening pulse, which we should under other circumstances welcome as favorable signs, but which, in diphtheria, are only too often the signs of coming death."*

Red and watery eyes, which appear corroded, the tears being acrid and more or less abundant; a cold perspiration, with coldness of the extremities; sinking, fainting turns, and stools containing bits or shreds of the false membrane, will be recognized as unfavorable symptoms.

Finally, epidemic peculiarities will modify your prognosis. As it prevails in certain seasons, and in certain districts of country, the type may be a very malignant one, and most examples of diphtheria prove rapidly fatal, even without the appearance of those symptoms usually denominated mortal. If it should be your misfortune, gentlemen, ever to encounter such an epidemic, pray do not fail to make a liberal discount upon the ordinary results of your practice, when you find yourselves weighing the probabilities *pro* and *contra* for your patient's recovery.

---

* Dr. E. L. Ormerod, London Lancet, March, 1862, p. 167.

LECTURE IV.

NATURE AND ETIOLOGY OF DIPHTHERIA.—*Should be classed among zymotic disorders.—The result of a specific epidemic virus.—Modifying circumstances favorable to its development.—The specific cause diffused through the atmosphere.—Inoculation.—Death of eminent medical men from.—Diphtheritic deposit upon a wounded finger.—Ditto upon old ulcers, the toes, etc.—Bretonneau's peculiar views.*—IS DIPHTHERIA CONTAGIOUS?—*Opinions of several of the most eminent authorities upon this subject.—Conclusions based upon these views and upon the author's own experience.*—ANATOMICAL CHARACTERISTICS.—*The formation of the pseudo-membrane.—The parasitic theory.—Reproduction of the membrane.—Differs from other heterologous growths.—Dissolution of the blood, the source of the general symptoms.—The true specific lesion, the result of the epidemic cause.—This cause produces its peculiar consequences by impairing the cell-life of the solid.—Dynamical susceptibilities, toxical and remedial, of the epithelial cell.*—SEQUELÆ, *paralytic, glandular and miscellaneous.*

GENTLEMEN :—

In the present Lecture, I shall first direct your attention to the study of the

Nature and Etiology of Diphtheria.—There appears but little doubt that this disease is zymotic in its nature, that its characteristic symptoms are the fruit of blood-poisoning, and that its first cause is to be found in a specific virus, which vitiates and depraves that most important fluid, and through this, the structure and function of certain solids. The arguments in favor of a specific cause for the diphtheria, are based upon the facts that it has traversed the world as an epidemic, and that the pathological lesion, which is its prominent characteristic, is as peculiar to this disease, as the specific affection of Peyer's patches is to typhoid fever, or the cutaneous eruption which goes through the three distinct and successive developments of papule, vesicle and pustule, is of the variola.

You are already aware that zymotic diseases are produced in one of two ways: the poison is either introduced into the blood from without the body, or it is produced within the organism by the retention or absorption of those post-organic matters in the circulatory current, which should have been set free at the various excretory surfaces. But these toxicohæmic causes frequently act in harmony. The specific epidemic virus taints the blood. The tissues drink from an impure fountain, and are themselves poisoned. The resorption which must occur in consequence of the destructive metamorphosis of the solids, is a second and very malignant source of increased danger to the welfare of the organism. The little leaven which first circulated in the life-giving current, is become the nidus of disease, and has developed a train of the most serious consequences. The adynamic and putrid symptoms of malignant diphtheria originate in this twin-headed source of blood-poisoning.

Zymotic diseases, of whatever variety, are engrafted upon organisms which are susceptible to the influence of their specific cause. This cause must find a soil which is congenial and favorable to its development, as well in diphtheria as in scarlatina, rubeola, or erysipelas. While, therefore, certain varíéties of climate and constitution render many persons exempt from attacks of diphtheria, yet other conditions are known to be favorable to its existence and spread. All those physical impurities of air, water, and food, which deprave the vitality of the human organism, tend to predispose individuals and communities brought under the immediate influence of its specific zymotic cause.

Marshy and aguish districts furnish an atmosphere favorable to its development. Diphtheria may, indeed, prevail in the higher localities, but, when this happens, there will always be found some especial local reason for it. The inhabitants may have been so weakened by previous disease, impure food, or other anti-hygienic means, as to render a majority of them susceptible to epidemic causes of the diphtheria. It appears, however, judging from the general prevalence and greater fatality of the disease in some portions of the Great West, that paludal influences do furnish a more congenial soil for the diphtheritic seed. Not a few of my professional friends, who are located in portions of the country in which intermittent and remittent diseases have formerly prevailed, have spoken of the virulent nature of epidemics of the diphtheria occurring within the range of their observation. All the children in some families, and in many cases the adults also, would be seized, and, without the greatest care on their part, sacrificed to this relentless destroyer. In many sections, not a family, of which some of its members had not been seriously ill, would escape.

Certain other meteorological conditions minister, also, to the spread of epidemic diphtheria. As a rule, it is less apt to prevail in a uniformly cold winter than in the summer months. Where, however, as during the present winter, in this latitude, the weather is cloudy, and the atmosphere more humid, the season more capricious than usual, we find the conditions of its prevalence supplied. In the history of particular epidemics of this disease, we are struck with the frequent exceptions to a general rule regarding this very matter of the influence of varieties and vicissitudes of temperature and season as modifying them. While the cold frosts of winter usually put an effectual stop to the extension of this class of diseases, there have been instances recorded in which the virulence and general spread of epidemic diphtheria were increased thereby. Sometimes, its more aggravated type is seen in an atmosphere which is rare, dry, and of uniform temperature. Again, it is most malignant in moist and rainy weather, especially in the spring, when "the frost is coming out of the ground."

If the air has been contaminated with animal or organic effluvia, it is remarked that the disease prevails in a more aggravated form. Besides, if the individual attacked is of a scrofulous or rheumatic habit, a victim, in short, to any of the predisponents of disease which are recognized in the various dyscrasiæ, the specific exciting cause of the diphtheria will be more certain to develop in them its own legitimate and peculiar consequences. For this reason, in cities especially, it prevails more generally among the lower classes. In this it resembles the yellow fever, Asiatic cholera, and, indeed, every species of zymotic disorder. In such subjects the vital fluids are more readily impressed by the epidemic cause, for the reason that they are more depraved in character, in consequence of the anti-hygienic conditions to which they have been subjected.

We are therefore led to infer the existence of a specific but invisible cause for the diphtheria, which, in order to the production of its own specific fruits, must first be introduced into the blood. The avenues through which it finds entrance may vary in different cases. The respiratory and the alimentary mucous membranes present surfaces which may absorb it along with the oxygen and the food which are furnished. Or it may be taken into the circulation through cutaneous surfaces which have been denuded of their epidermis, as in a scratch, an open wound, or an ulcer.

This epidemic virus appears to float in a more or less attenuated form through the atmosphere. A strong argument for its specific nature and properties is found in the fact that persons who are in health may be inoculated with the poison of diphtheria from one who is ill with it, and that the train of consequences which follow are as characteristic of this disease as are those which result from inoculation in small-pox, or from syphilization. All that appears necessary in order to cause the disorder at will is to introduce some of the secretions from the throat of a diphtheritic subject into the mouth and fauces of one who is susceptible, and the disease is forthwith engrafted upon his organism. There are several published examples which confirm this statement. I have translated you one from Trousseau :*

"One of our lamented hospital *confrères*, whose name is familiar to all, and whose works are in the hands of many of you, M. Valleix, had the professional care of a child ill with membranous angina. The attack aws not of a very grave nature, and the child recovered, thanks to the prompt treatment employed by our unfortunate colleague. One day, while examining the patient's throat, Valleix received into his mouth a little of the saliva which had been ejected in an attempt to cough. He contracted the disease. The next day he recognized the presence of a little pellicular concretion upon one of his tonsils; anticipated by a light febrile movement. At the end of a few hours, both tonsils and the uvula were covered by false membranes. Soon an abundant secretion of serous liquid drained from the nose; the glands of the neck, and the cellular tissue of the neck and of the inferior part of the jaw, were considerably swollen; there had been some delirium, and in forty-eight hours Valleix died without having presented any symptoms of laryngeal complication."

Trousseau records two other similar examples. A surgeon performed tracheotomy in a severe case of diphtheritic croup. The blood flowing into the trachea, he became alarmed, applied his mouth to the wound in order to suck away the blood from the air-tube, and thus became inoculated with the virus. Forty-eight hours later he died of malignant diphtheria. The third case was very similar, the victim of the inoculation living in all some three or four days.

In our own country, Professor Frick, of the University of Maryland, contracted the disease while performing tracheotomy upon a negro woman who was dying with epidemic diphtheria. He operated on Tuesday, and died of the same affection on the following Sunday. Dr. Cooke, of Brooklyn, N. Y., received the virus into his system, probably through the lungs, or it may have been in some other way, while administering to the relief of a diphtheritic patient, and died in about a week.

My friend Dr. E. McAffee, of this State, related to me last evening the case of a woman who, in attempting to force open

* *Clinique Medicale*, Tome I, p. 335.

the mouth of her child ill with diphtheria, had her finger slightly wounded by the teeth of the little patient. After some six or seven days had elapsed, the doctor found that a distinct and unmistakable diphtheritic membrane had formed over the abrasion.

Examples are recorded in which this deposit has been known to cover the surface of old ulcers, like a patch, the edges of the new tissue overlapping upon the margins of the sound skin. Sometimes stringy shreds hang out of them, the diphtheritic poison not affecting the organism to such a degree as to develop any throat symptoms, or indeed to produce the least constitutional disturbance whatever.

M. Bretonneau records that, "a boy with frost-bites of his foot, happening to use a bath that had been employed for a diphtheritic patient, his great toe became the seat of diphtheritic exudation, which caused it to be extremely painful." In the *Memoirs dê Med. et Chirurgie Militaire*, Paris, 1854, we find an account of a soldier who contracted the disease by using a tea-spoon which had been in the mouth of a diphtheritic patient.

These, gentlemen, are the data upon which the opinion is based that diphtheria is due to a specific invisible virus which, introduced into the blood, developes its own legitimate and characteristic fruits; and these are the reasons why we cannot endorse the view of those authorities who regard it but a modification of croup, of ordinary angina, of scarlatina or of measles. We have seen that the poison, once introduced into the circulation, gives rise to an identical lesion, as truly as does that peculiar to variola, scarlatina, syphilis, or even hydrophobia. If the diphtheria were a modified form of either of the afore-named disorders, they should be mutually convertible, and, especially in case of the exanthemata named, one attack should always exempt the patient from a second. We have seen that genuine diphtheria affords no protection from the scarlatina, any more than the scarlatina does from measles, or measles from small-pox.

Indeed, the frequency of second attacks of diphtheria

occurring in the same person precludes the possibility that the disease is essentially the same in nature with either of the exanthemata. Diphtheria may occur the third time in the same person.

M. Bretonneau believed the diphtheria to be a local disease, resembling croup, but inclined to spread itself by continuity of tissue and thus to affect the general organism secondarily. I have already given my reasons for the non-acceptance of this view of its nature. There is the most conclusive evidence that the system is primarily affected, while the local lésions are a secondary result of diphtheritic poisoning. Whether or not there shall be fever from the onset of the attack, there is token of the presence and effect of a putrescent poison in the blood. The adynamia, and extreme prostration, the manifest malignancy of the disorder, the offensive breath, the very look of the patient, impress one with the conviction that changes are taking place in the circulating fluid which render it unfit for purposes of nutrition. Its solids are more or less disintegrated, and its lymph de-vitalized. In its course, it taints the tissues, and in return is corrupted by them. It furnishes a depraved plasma from which the glandular epithelium is to elaborate all the various bodily secretions, and so clogs the excretory outlets as to defeat the ends of their function.

This septic condition of the blood occasions the liability to hæmorrhage, and the abrasion and ulceration of the mucous membranes in the diphtheria. It also induces the paralytic and suppurative sequelæ of the disease. It aims a blow at the functions of assimilation, respiration and innervation. In brief, unless the effects of the specific virus are in some way counteracted, or the virus is eliminated, disastrous consequences are almost certain to follow.

Is it Contagious?—Certain eminent authorities entertain and advocate the opinion that the diphtheria is contagious. It certainly prevails as an epidemic, frequently attacks entire families, and in a few instances would appear to have been conveyed and communicated from one neighborhood to another as contagious affections are sometimes known to be.

For the peace of community, and your own satisfaction as practitioners, it is important, if possible, to settle the question of the contagiousness of diphtheria. That this disease is due to the presence of an especial virus which has been first introduced into the blood, there appears but little doubt. That there are persons, and children especially, in all the walks of life, among the rich and the poor, remote from all anti-hygienic influences, or exposed to them, who are alike susceptible to the action of this specific poison, there is no question. The diphtheria may be engrafted upon a scrofulous or a rheumatic diathesis. Syphilis may act as a predisponent of the disease. All the children in a family may be seized with it, or a number of them may escape. Like the scarlatina, it selects its victims from particular families in the same neighborhood.

Nearly all the French authorities agree that the diphtheria is contagious. Bretonneau, Guersant, Miguel, Trousseau and others, are of this opinion. Jurine and Brichetau oppose this view; while Rilliet and Barthez think it more feebly contagious than most eruptive diseases. Bretonneau decided that diphtheria is not transmitted by the atmosphere, but is always the result of inoculation, requiring, however, a damp atmosphere for its development.

The English and American writers differ upon this question. Possibly, because he would not raise a doubt of the identity of croup and diphtheria, West does not commit himself to either view. Dr. Edward Ballard* advocates the contagiousness of diphtheria, for the following reasons:

1. "Infectious diseases habitually spread in families they invade. Out of 47 families there were only 15 in which the other members all remained healthy.

2. "As a rule, it spread in the houses it invaded chiefly among those members of the several families who were most closely in communication.

3. "In no case where separation from the sick person has been effected early in the disease, have I noticed that it has spread to the separated individuals. In one case where communication had been allowed for three days before separation,

* Medical Times and Gazette, for July 23d, 1859.

a child was seized with diphtheria on the sixth day of removal from home."

Dr. Ballard quotes several examples in proof of its contagiousness.

Dr. Wm. Jenner, in the Clinical Lecture to which I have already alluded, remarks, "That it is contagious, but requires for its propagation either complete exposure to the contagious principle, or predisposition on the part of those receiving it, and that the latter is probably by far the more important of the two conditions of its development." And, in a foot-note, he adds, "There is not a shadow of ground for the belief that the disease can be carried by the clothes, etc., from one house to another."

Dr. Ranking,* in one of his lectures on diphtheria says: "My own conviction is that it is infectious to a limited degree; by which I mean that when patients are accumulated in small, ill-ventilated rooms, the disease is likely to be communicated; but I do not fear that, like scarlatina or erysipelas, it may be propagated in spite of all sanitary precautions, still less that the infection can be conveyed by the clothes or persons of those who visit or superintend the patients. That it commonly spreads through the family once invaded is to be attributed, in some degree, to the persistence of the same cause as originated the first case. What that cause is, it is difficult to determine."

Dr. D. F. Condie† writes: "I have not met with a single fact that would lead me to suspect that diphtheria is susceptible of being propagated by contagion. Whenever I have been able to investigate properly the circumstances which have been adduced in evidence of the contagious character of the disease, I have invariably found them to be simply cases in which the diphtheria has successively made its appearance in individuals who had visited or who were residents of a location in which it was at the time prevailing, and who, in consequence, were equally exposed to the same malaria, the same epidemic cause by which the disease was generated in those previously attacked, and from whom it was supposed to be contracted by those who sickened subsequently. In all these instances it was almost certain that in those who took the disease it was generated by a common atmospheric cause, which, we admit,

---

* London Lancet, January 15, 1857.

† Proceedings of Phila. Co. Med. Society, 1862.

was more active in certain localities than in others within the sphere of the epidemic influence, from the want of due ventilation, overcrowding and other unfavorable hygienic conditions."

In his Memoirs on Diphtheria, published by the New Sydenham Society, we find M. Daviot* makes the following remarks: "Like other diseases which assume this (epidemic) character, it only manifests itself in those localities and individuals which have the most affinity for it. Springing from an alteration in the constituent elements of the atmosphere, an alteration unknown in its essence but appreciable in its effects, it is propagated through the medium of that fluid. * * * * * A great number of persons were struck by the epidemic a few days after arriving in the infected places, and without having communicated with any patient."

Dr. H. C. Preston† says: "I conclude that diphtheria is essentially an epidemic, non-contagious disease, rarely in certain favoring localities becoming endemic by concentration of the epidemic influence."

My friend Dr. Wm. Todd Helmuth,‡ quotes Dr. Preston's conclusion, and endorses it, in the following language: "This is, no doubt, a fact, for there are few physicians who have paid attention to the subject who have not, either from personal observation or from the perusal of some medical periodicals, noticed several in one family, in one house, or in one particular locality, successively affected."

Dr. Jas. Wynne, in a paper on Diphtheria, read before the N. Y. Academy of Medicine, January, 1861, concludes his remarks upon this subject as follows: "The appearance of the disease at various and remote parts of the American Continent about the same period of time, and the absolute impossibility of communication between the first cases of the disease in the various places where it has manifested itself, clearly establish the fact that its introduction into any locality where it has appeared is not due to contagion. The writer is inclined to the belief that under certain favorable conditions, after being introduced, it is susceptible of transmission by contagion."

---

* Memoirs on Diphtheria, (New Sydenham Society) London, 1857.

† U. S. Journal of Homœopathy, Vol. I, p. 236.

‡ A Treatise on Diphtheria, its Nature, Pathology, etc., 1862, p. 30.

Dr. J. P. Dake* records: "From all my osbervations, I am satisfied that it is not contagious—that it does not spread from one person to another; but that all imbibe its peculiar cause, or, if you please, *materia peccans*, from a common source."

Dr. Monckton† is thus explicit: "No decisive instance of its communicability has come before me; on the contrary, I have seen it attack individuals only, in a family of liable persons, much more frequently than I think scarlet fever would have done. My own conviction is, that diphtheria is epidemic, endemic (*id est* largely affected by locality), and non-contagious, or, if contagious at all, vastly less so than scarlet fever, from which last it is very distinct."

Mr. Ernest Hart‡ gives the following somewhat poetical version of the subject: "Zymotic in its nature, it (diphtheria) tends to fasten upon whomsoever is debilitated by previous disease, or by a constitution naturally feeble and artificially effeminized, or whose vitality is lowered by the depressing influences of luxury, indolence and inactivity; and the habitual defiance of physical and hygienic laws, which is so frequent an element in fashionable life. Hence individual causes come into play, and introduce this associate of the poor into the palaces and mansions of the great, which they so often fringe. Diphtheria finds there its victims, pale and anæmic, or grossly sanguineous, and unhealthily excited."

I have quoted thus extensively from the writings of the most distinguished physicians in order, if possible, to sustain those conclusions which my own somewhat limited experience had enabled me to reach. Indeed, it is only through comparison of the results of extended observation among medical men who practice in various quarters of the globe, and have met with all the diversified types and peculiarities of the diphtheria, that the question of its contagiousness can ever be settled. The following inferences, I apprehend, are clearly deducible from the foregoing opinions.

1. Diphtheria arises from a specific invisible cause, which,

* North American Journal of Hom., Vol. X, p. 425.

† Medical Times and Gazette, Feb. 26, 1857.

‡ Diphtheria, its History, etc., by Ernest Hart, London, 1859.

in order to produce its legitimate pathological fruits, must first be introduced into the blood.

2. The means for the introduction of this virus into the blood are two in number, viz: through the respiration and by inoculation.

3. We cannot conceive of an epidemic cause which fails to occasion more or less contamination of the atmosphere. Local circumstances may concentrate such a taint, and thus render susceptible persons in community more liable to contract the disease from breathing this atmosphere.

4. In exceptional cases the diphtheria may spread in this manner, by a thorough poisoning of the air which is breathed; but, as a rule, it is much more feebly contagious than either of the eruptive fevers. There is no evidence that it is ever conveyed by *fomites.*

5. The only known method of successful inoculation is that a portion of the vitiated secretions from either the mucous membranes or the skin of a diphtheritic subject be applied to an absorbent surface.

6. Both these methods of communicating the disease will fail unless the individual constitution and local habits and surroundings of the subject afford a congenial soil in which the specific cause may develop its specific effects.

Anatomical Characteristics.—It is the universal sentiment of medical writers that the pseudo-membrane is to be regarded as the more prominent pathological feature of the diphtheria. With the method of its formation we are not quite familiar. Some authorities believe that the first step in the process is due to the presence of a parasitic fungus, which acts as the exciting cause of abnormal changes in the structure of the epithelial and endermic surfaces. Dr. Laycock* gives a detailed description of the diphtheritic oidium or mould, which, he says, "acts like all its tribe, as an irritant, inducing increased formation of epithelial scales, and effusion of mucous exudation, corpuscles or plasma; intermingled among which are the

* Clinical Lecture on Diphtheria, etc., London, 1859.

sporules, and the mycelium of the microscopic fungus; the whole constituting a pellicle or membrane, varying in thickness." We cannot, however, place very great reliance upon this view of the origin of the peculiar diphtheritic lesion. Dr. Laycock's opinions are founded upon observations made in a single case of the disease, in which the microscopical fungus, the oidium albicans, may have been accidentally, and not necessarily, present.

Greenhow says, upon this point: "Low forms of cryptogamic plants are occasionally found on the exudation, which gave rise to the belief that the disease is of parasitic origin. This opinion is disproved by the facts, that on the one hand, the supposed parasite is not invariably present in diphtheria, and on the other, that it is frequently found on unhealthy mucous surfaces, which are not of a diphtheritic nature."

Other and older authorities, among whom is the celebrated Vogel, have recognized this parasite as frequently present in all the various lesions of the oral and pharyngeal mucous membranes.

One thing appears certain. The adventitious formation is the fruit of derangement in the tissue-making processes which are proper to the parts affected. Now, whether the cause acts directly or indirectly upon the epithelial or epidermic cells, in order to produce this effect, we do not know, nor is it of material consequence that we should. If we are not prepared to accept the parasitic theory of the source of this lesion, we shall be compelled to refer it to a disorder of the internal nutritive processes. The physiological law of waste and repair is perverted, in so far as the diseased structure is concerned. A new tissue is indeed constructed in lieu of the old one, but its form and function are not the same. It is heteroplastic and not homœoplastic: formed after a pathological, and not after the primitive type.

"*Diphtheria* prefers a location upon the tonsils, the pharynx, the veil of the palate, the baccal cavity, properly speaking; *muguet* occupies almost exclusively the latter, and the digestive organs. The *ulcero-membranous stomatitis* attacks one side of the mouth, upon the internal face of the cheek, or the alveolar ridge. *Stomato-mercurial concretions* are deposited upon the mucous membrane, covering the gums, the *genale*, or the tongue. *Pultaceous angina* causes the mucous membrane upon the tonsils and pharynx to become red and dry. * * *

"Diphtheria is, of all pseudo-membranous affections, that in which the plastic product is the most promptly reproduced, in which it spreads over a more extensive surface, and is manifested upon several points at the same time."*

The diphtheritic false membrane differs in many respects from all other heterologous growths. The adhesions which attend inflammation of serous structures, are more firmly organized, fibrinous, and have the power to attach themselves, by either or both their sides, to another surface. The diphtheritic membrane is never attached to subjacent integument, excepting upon one side, and is less firmly constructed because of the variety of surface upon which it is located, the disordered nutritive and type forces of which have produced it, and the low, putrid condition of the blood which always characterizes the disease.

The pseudo-membrane of croup has not only its definite location upon the laryngo-tracheal mucous surfaces, never being found elsewhere, but the membrane itself is said to differ in composition from that produced in diphtheria. Dr. Madden† believes that the membrane in croup is fibrinous, and not albuminous as in diphtheria. I have here, gentlemen, a tracheal cast, which was expectorated by a little patient with membranous croup. You will remark the firmness of its organization, its thickness, its elasticity, and the evident depressions upon its attached surface formed by the tracheal cartilages.

It is interesting to inquire into the manner in which the specific septic cause of the diphtheria produces its peculiar results. Under all its forms and varieties, the disease is essentially the same. In one family we may have pharyngeal,

---

* *Recherches Cliniques et Anatomiques sur les Affections Pseudo-Membraneuses, etc., Par A. Laboulbène*, Paris, 1861, p. 29.

† British Journal of Hom., June, 1861.

laryngeal, palpæbral, cutaneous and vulvular deposit of pseudo-membrane. "It is with the diphtheria as with variola, which, confluent or distinct, mild or malignant, is always variola."*

I have already referred to changes in the blood as a marked and necessary consequence of diphtheritic, as of all other varieties of zymotic poisoning. These alterations consist substantially in the breaking down of its crasis, so as effectually to interfere with the organizing processes of the economy. In brief, the blood is de-fibrinated in diphtheria, as in typhus fever, malignant scarlatina, erysipelas, scorbutus and sunstroke. M. Millard† reports that its color is changed; instead of being of a red tint, which is more or less shaded, it is brown, resembling the juice of prunes or of liquorice, and staining the fingers as does the sepia. M. Peter, in a memoir published in 1859, compares this discolored blood to water which contains soot.

As you would anticipate, the circulation of this depraved fluid is calculated to engender disease in the various solids. The general manifestations of abnormal action find herein their original cause. Many of the symptoms and sequelæ of diphtheria, as for example, the disordered innervation, the vitiated secretions, the albuminuria, the anæmia, the hæmorrhages, the abscesses, are caused by a depraved condition of the blood. This it is which constitutes the diphtheritic cachexia, as it is termed, of which, indeed, the local exudation and pseudo-membranous deposit are merely the characteristic features. We thus find little difficulty in explaining the origin of the constitutional symptoms of this disease, but is this general cause alone sufficient to account for the production of the specific anatomical lesion which characterizes the diphtheria?

That the false membrane in diphtheria is principally albuminous, or but slightly fibrinous, there can be no doubt. That we are to infer from this single fact that "the disease consists

---

* Trousseau, *Clinique Medicale*, Tome I, p. 364.

† *Thèse Inaugurale sur la Trachetomie dans le cas de Croup*, Paris, 1858.

in an albuminous condition of the blood,"* is not clear, to my own mind at least. If we grant that Lehmann's chemical theory, "That fibrin is produced by the oxidation of albumen in the æration of the blood," is correct; that, in many cases of diphtheria the deposits upon and within the glottis interfere very materially with the freedom and thoroughness of the respiratory act; that diphtheritic heart-clots and deposits are always found in the pulmonic side of that viscus; and that albuminuria argues an excess in the relative proportion of albumen contained in the blood; what do these facts establish? Simply, that if we attribute the especial lesion of diphtheria to this source alone, we have mistaken an effect for the cause.

Let me illustrate. The blood is organizable, and not in itself organized, as we say that building materials are organizable, capable of being organized into an edifice. In the healthy state, its fibrin may coagulate spontaneously, when withdrawn from the body, by the escape of the ammonia which held it in solution, but this change in its form is as different from true histogenetic organization as is the hardening of the mortar-mass in the sun different from its solidification as an integral part of a building. The plasma is a concentrated solution of the bodily structures. Albumen and fibrin are its more important elements. But these elements are as incapable of independent tissue formation as are building materials to incorporate themselves into an edifice.

This view implies the necessity for an operative constructing force, which shall preside over the organization of the plasma into tissues, nervous, muscular, mucous, osseous, ligamentous, or what not. It implies a refutation of the old doctrine of "elective affinity." It corrects the sentiment that "blood makes tissue," for it recognizes that tissues are *made from the blood*, by regular process of organization, and through the direct agency of organs which are endowed in part with this especial function.

These organs are the cells which aggregate the bodily

* Helmuth, *loc. cit.*, p. 63.

textures. Each tissue has its characteristic cells, each of which has its own form and function. Indeed, the very varieties of form and function are due to this anatomical arrangement. Now, every one of these little organs is endowed with the three varieties of force which Virchow styles Nutritive, Formative, and Functional. The first presides over its nutrition, progressive and destructive. The second preserves the characteristic type or form of the cell-structure. The third, its peculiar function, as distinguished from that of all the remaining textures.

When I produce a species of false membrane at will, as may sometimes be done, by means of a blister of Spanish flies applied upon the surface, or by giving cantharides, tartar emetic, the bichromate of potassa, or the proto-iodide of mercury, internally, you will not suppose it necessary to dissolve all the fibrin which is contained in the blood in order to give rise to a local lesion. Neither is it probable that such a means would retard the physiological change of albuminose into fibrin which is going on in the mesenteric and other lymphatic glands. I employ a local agent in the one case, and local results are manifest. The specific force of cantharis has so overcome the cell-forces that the healthy nutrition, formation and function of the enveloping texture are deranged. Remove the blister, evacuate the contained serum, let the epidermis exfoliate, and a heteroplastic structure is supplied in lieu of a true and genuine scarf-skin or cuticle. A drop of cantharides applied upon the mucous membrane produces the same identical changes.

Administered internally, the other agents named are conveyed by the blood to those epithelial surfaces for which each has its especial affinity. Arrived at its destination, each produces its own characteristic local consequences, without direct reference to the general organism. The preparations of mercurius find the squamous cells upon the buccal and superior alimentary surfaces particularly susceptible to their toxical influence. The bichromate of potassa and the tartrate of antimony appear to impress their specific forces upon the ciliated epithelium lining the respiratory organs, in preference to those covering the alimentary mucous membrane. Each impresses the solids through the blood, but the blood-tide itself has no especial relation to one of these textures considered apart from the other. As it may convey nourishment that will be received by the one and rejected by the other, so it may supply a specific toxical force to which the one shall be vulnerable while the other is not.

Here is an explanation of the source of epidemic varieties of the diphtheria, noted by various authors, from the time of old Dr. Bard, or Bretonneau, until the present. And here also, the key to remedial susceptibilities, in other words to the special therapeutics of the disease.

We conclude, therefore, that, while the more general and constitutional symptoms of diphtheria evidence a depraved and de-fibrinated condition of the blood, the local lesion is the result of inoculation with an epidemic germ or virus which is endowed with a specific force, which has a remarkable and fatal predilection for epithelial structures. The necessity of this specific cause is shown in the fact that while a stroke of lightning, or an attack of typhus, of scorbutus, or of malignant scarlatina, or erysipelas, may so dissolve the crasis of the blood as to render it incapable of coagulation when withdrawn from the body, and also produce many of the general symptoms common to zymotic disorders, they are not characterized by the formation of false membranes upon any of the free surfaces.

It has not been demonstrated that an asphyxiated state of system is necessarily followed by exudative inflammation of the pharyngeal and tracheal mucous membrane. In brief, those structural disorganizations upon epithelial surfaces, which are peculiar to the diphtheria, to croup, and to stomatitis, are as certainly and clearly traceable to the operation of specific disease-producing forces, as is the eruption of small-pox, measles, or scarlet-fever each to its own specific and especial cause. The blood may convey this force to the particular tissue implicated, but the pseudo-membrane in the one case, and the eruptive lesion in the other, must necessarily result from a disorder in the cell-life of the solid.

Sequelæ.—Among all the various sequelæ of diphtheria the disorders of innervation are the more frequent and interesting. As has already been said, the nervous centres are poisoned, and their function more or less seriously deranged. In some cases patients will recover from the more acute symptoms of diphtheria with an affection of the spinal cord, or its enveloping membranes. They will complain of pains in the occipital region, extending along down the spine, it may be, throughout its whole length. These pains are acute and lancinating in character, greatly aggravated by motion, and accompanied by various disorders in the two sets of nervous filaments which have their origin in the medulla spinalis.

Where the posterior or sensory filaments are chiefly affected, there will result a marked disorder of the temperature, as well as of the sensibility of surfaces to which these filaments are supplied. The patient recovers from the diphtheria with an extraordinary sensitiveness to cool air. Moving the bed-clothing, the opening or closing of the door, rapid motion of an attendant in his chamber, a hint that the room is too warm, any little occurrence which may serve to direct attention to his individual feelings in regard of temperature, chills him. His skin does not feel cold to the touch of another, yet he complains of positive suffering from this sensation. Even after he has so far convalesced as to leave his room he may experience this symptom. Sometimes, however, the opposite state is the cause of complaint. The patient is the victim of flushes of heat which keep him always aglow, and serve to interfere with his rest and exercise. The sensation as of excess of heat in the skin which is experienced may be real or imaginary, may be relieved by a free flow of perspiration, or pass off without any increased escape of sweat or of urine. In either case, it implies a derangement in the function of the sensory filaments which is due to a poisoning of the nerve-centre.

A species of paralysis of these filaments is frequently met with after diphtheria. The skin upon one part or another, or indeed upon the whole exterior of the body, is less sensitive than in health. Touch is less acute. The more ordinary stimulii do not awaken the perceptions. Sensation may be partially or wholly suspended. The skin feels numb, or perhaps tingles unpleasantly. Sometimes there is formication. Again, sensibility seems almost gone, and after a brief interval is resumed, but in an acute degree. He is become super-sensitive. At one visit you will find him complaining that his extremities feel as if they were dead, or did not belong to him. The feet seem like stuffed cushions. The limbs are indeed attached to his body, but feel to him as if they belonged to some one else. If you pinch or prick the skin, he experiences pain in proportion as the lesion of these sensory filaments is more or less profound. At another time his suffering is evident. The same surfaces are become morbidly sensitive, his limbs ache like the tooth-ache, and the least touch may give rise to the most severe pain.

This derangement may last for a few days only, or it may persist for weeks or even months, the local anæsthesia wearing away as the general health and vigor are restored. Some patients are strangely affected. I have met with one case in which this species of paralysis was confined to the little finger of the left hand, and did not entirely disappear until six months subsequent to the attack of diphtheria. In another, the sensibility of the right foot was lost. Instances are recorded in which the sense of Taste, itself a modification of Touch, was absent for many weeks.

Trousseau has shown that a loss of sensibility in the velum palati may occasion difficult articulation and deglutition, the fluids which are drunken returning through the nose, and choking sensations in an attempt to swallow solids, due to a violent spasmodic action of the pharyngeal muscles. When either the pharynx or the larynx are paralyzed, the voice has a nasal twang, and there will be more or less dysphagia. The taking of cold drinks will sometimes occasion this spasm, even where months have elapsed since the acute attack has subsided.

In many cases the function of the pneumogastric nerve is

impaired, and the patient convalesces with evident disorder of the lungs or stomach. In those who are predisposed to consumption or to dyspepsia, this paralysis may prove an exciting cause of subsequent and serious illness. I have treated several cases of asthenic pneumonia due to this cause. Whenever there is an abnormal play of the pharyngeal muscles, great feebleness and irregularity of the heart's action, and a more or less obstinate vomiting, after an attack of diphtheria, you may be assured the par vagum is in a measure paralyzed.

Nervous dyspnœa, with intractable emesis, of the character which Goodfellow styles "explosive vomiting," are symptoms of albuminuria also, and may sometimes be recognized as the result of uræmic poisoning.

Paralysis of the motor nervous filaments is by no means an infrequent sequel of diphtheria. This is shown in the extreme general debility which follows even in the milder cases. The patient walks with difficulty, totters, reels as if intoxicated, complains of vertigo when in an upright position, and perhaps his hand trembles as in *paralysis agitans*. The tongue may be so paralyzed as to render articulation difficult. Or there may be hemiplegia, or paraplegia.

One of my little patients convalesced from diphtheria with paralysis of both arms. The muscles of the back, or those of the neck may be powerless. Now and then, especially among adults, wry-neck results. Two sets of muscles in a limb sometimes become subject to irregular contraction. The flexors and extensors of the fore-arm may afford this symptom. The former contract at once and firmly, and the extensors are left powerless; afterward the latter may suffer the same tonic rigidity, and the flexors be temporarily helpless.

Irregular muscular action may produce a species of St. Vitus' dance, with which some patients recover from diphtheria. Tenesmus of the bladder or rectum may supervene upon the same disease. Dysmenorrhœa is more frequent during and subsequent to an epidemic of diphtheria than at other times. Pains, and aching of the limbs, especially upon motion, with stiffness of the joints, are among its more familiar sequelæ.

The arms are, as it were, nerveless, and the legs can scarcely carry the body, their movements being uncertain and tottering.

These varieties of diphtheritic paralysis are of exceeding interest. In certain epidemics a majority of those who are seized with diphtheria become paralytic. It is by no means the least interesting feature of this class of sequelæ that the paralysis is in general not so permanent as when it follows other affections. Concerning its source and significance, physicians are not agreed. A majority refer to blood-poisoning as its most manifest cause, and believe the non-elimination of urinary matters will explain the paralytic phenomena. Trousseau and others oppose this theory. I have already given you my own views upon the subject.

If you will bear in mind the remark of the celebrated Marshall Hall, that, "In cerebral paralysis the irritability of the muscular fibre is *augmented*; in spinal paralysis it becomes gradually more and more *diminished*; while, in ganglionic paralysis, if complete, it may become *extinct*," you will have a key to the seat and severity of the lesion which many physicians do not possess.

Besides the nervous sequelæ already mentioned, there are yet others. The nerves of special sense may be paralyzed. Amaurosis, or palsy of the optic nerve, is a not unfrequent result. The patient becomes in a measure blind, cannot distinguish the letters on a printed page, or objects across the chamber. The pupil is widely dilated, and bodies float before the eye. Sometimes there will be more or less squinting. In other cases, one or both the pupils remain permanently dilated. This symptom recalls to mind the interesting pathological observation of Dr. Noyes,* who observed, by use of the ophthalmoscope, that the amaurosis which so frequently accompanies Bright's disease of the kidneys, is dependent upon a fatty degeneration of the retina; a state of things which may characterize the albuminuria of diphtheria.

Or the auditory filaments are functionally disordered. The hearing is thickened, or there may be real deafness, a result which is sometimes due to an extension of the inflammation from

* Bulletin of the N. Y. Academy of Medicine, Vol. I, p. 469.

the pharyngeal cavity, along the Eustachian tube to the middle ear, again to the tumefaction of the tonsils and cervical glands, and at other times to paralysis of the delicate filaments of the portio mollis.

The olfactory sense is much impaired, and, indeed, quite suspended, in many examples of diphtheria. Sometimes the sense of taste is not restored until considerable time has elapsed. It is a peculiarity of diphtheritic paralysis, however, that in all its forms, it is less persistent than one would at first suppose possible. *The amaurosis is but partial, incipient* as it were. The deafness, *in most examples, is not the result* of inflammation or organic lesion of the tympanum or other structures within the ear, and is therefore much less serious than that which attends or follows upon scarlatina. The senses of smell and of taste may be restored, the paralytic symptoms disappearing gradually.

The characteristic prostration, of which I have before spoken, may become a sequel to diphtheria. Convalescence from this disease is always lingering. The patient's system does not react, his vital energies run low, and there is constant danger of asthenic relapses to which he may finally succumb. Adults, in particular, frequently fail to regain their former strength and spirits, and are left in much the same physical condition as the soldiers who have suffered in camp from typhoid or intermittent fever, or the army diarrhœa.

This state of feebleness constitutes of itself a deplorable cachexia. Post-diphtheritic abscesses may form in various parts of the body. The tendency to glandular suppuration is indeed quite a characteristic sequel of diphtheria. One of my patients, a lad of ten years, survived twelve abscesses following an attack of this disease. The glands in the vicinity of the neck, or the conglobate glands of the lymphatic system, located upon various parts of the body, may suppurate and discharge. From most of these abscesses the pus which escapes is not healthy in appearance, but is thin, watery, sometimes offensive, almost always free in amount, and continues to ooze from the orifice, it may be for a number of days, without any change in its character. In a small ratio of cases, it is acrid, and sometimes ichorous.

Upon this subject, my friend Dr. L. Pratt remarks: *

"I remember one case in which the patient died after the throat symptoms had entirely subsided. He seemed to sink from pure debility. There was no healthy nutrition of the tissues; food did no good, although enough was taken. Another died from a swelling of the parotid; there was little constitutional disturbance, no fever, and no other lesion, and yet the patient died. Sometimes the sequelæ resemble those of scarlatina."

Abscesses of the ear are less frequent after diphtheria than subsequent to scarlatina, nevertheless, otorrhœa does sometimes result. Pulmonary abscess has been remarked as an occasional sequel of diphtheria. During convalescence, one of my private patients experienced a severe attack of orchitis. In some cases the skin is œdematous; in others, there are spots upon the surface, which appear to have lost their vitality, and become more or less gangrenous. Petechia and purpura may supervene,—the "spotted fever," as it is called. Patients now and then recover with a form of diarrhœa, or, it may be, of leucorrhœa, as secondary to the diphtheria. Urinary symptoms may remain among the last tokens of such an attack. Pectoral disorders, with cough and abnormal expectoration, frequently follow.

All of these symptoms and sequelæ point to the constitutional character of the diphtheria. There is no question but it is a systemic, and not merely a local disorder, which owes its essential characteristics to the presence of a species of parasitic growth, whether it be algous or fungous. It is zymotic in its origin, its characteristics, and its sequelæ. It is a disease *per se*, and not alone a dyscrasia. Like the typhoid fever, it has its general and its especial lesions, the one systemic and the other local.

To conclude, I must insist that the more thoroughly you are conversant with the detailed pathology of diphtheria, in all its bearings, the more practical and valuable will be your therapeutical deductions and prescriptions. My next Lecture will be devoted to the treatment of this disease.

---

* Trans. of Ill. Hom. Med. Association, 8th Annual Meeting, 1862. p. 63.

LECTURE V.

I.—THE CONSTITUTIONAL TREATMENT OF DIPHTHERIA.—FOR THE FEBRILE SYMPTOMS.—*Indications for Aconite.—Belladonna.—Gelseminum.—Rhus Toxicodendron.—Baptisia Tinctoria.—Bryonia Alb.*— FOR THE CEREBRAL DISORDER.—*Phosphorus.—Belladonna.—Opium.—Conium-mac.* —FOR THE MOUTH AND THROAT SYMPTOMS.—*Mercurius.—Iodine.—Mercurius-jodatus.—Cantharis.—Bi-chromate of Potassa.—Rhus Toxicodendron.—Iodide of Arsenic.—Baptisia tinct.—Nitric Acid.—Apis Mellifica.—Baryta Carbonica.—Belladonna.*—FOR THE ODOR OF THE BREATH. —FOR THE CORYZA.—DO. THE GASTRIC AND ALIMENTARY DISORDER.—*Nux Vomica.—Bryonia Alb.—Opium.—Veratrum Alb.—Phosphoric Acid.—Arsenicum Alb.—Nitric Acid. — Ars.-jodatus. — Merc.-jodatus.— Cantharis.*— FOR THE ERUPTION.—*Belladonna.—Rhus Tox.—Bryonia Alb. —Pulsatilla.—Nitric Acid.—Ars. Alb.—Cantharis.*—FOR THE URINARY DISORDER.—*Aconite.—Merc.-jodatus.—Cantharis.—Apis Mel.—Ammonia Acet.—Merc.-Corrosivus.—Phos. Acid.—Colchicum.*—FOR THE EXTREME DEBILITY.—*Remarkable Effect of Cantharides as a remedy for.*

II.—LOCAL TREATMENT.—*Effect of Chemical re-agents upon the false membrane.— Various local applications, gargles, etc.—Removal of Deposit.*

III.—HYGIENIC TREATMENT.—*Observations upon Diet, etc.*

IV.—SURGICAL DITTO.—*Tracheotomy.—Reasons why so frequently a fatal expedient.—Ablation of the Tonsils.—Tubing the Larynx.*—CONCLUSION.

GENTLEMEN :—

I shall divide the treatment of Diphtheria into I. Constitutional; II. Local; III. Hygienic; and IV. Surgical.

I.—CONSTITUTIONAL TREATMENT.

The analysis of the symptoms of diphtheria which we have made, has not alone a pathological, but also a therapeutical value. Let us follow the same order of investigation in deciding upon the most appropriate constitutional treatment for this disease.

For the Febrile Symptoms.—In those milder epidemics in which, although there is a more decided febrile disorder, there is a less persistent derangement of the functions of the skin and of the kidneys, than in the diphtheria maligna, Aconite is a valuable remedy. Its well-known power for the relief of simple fevers would lead us to expect the best results from its employment. It may be given with the hope of relieving capillary engorgement of the mucous surface of the throat and faucial cavity, the frequent pulse, and the more marked symptoms of a febrile paroxysm. Many practitioners think it an indispensable remedy in the treatment of both varieties of diphtheria; but this appears to be an unwarrantable generalization on their part.

In the treatment of the early stage of all the exanthemata, prior to the appearance of the eruption, you will discover that it is almost impossible to promote a free flow of the sensible perspiration or of the urine. The fever is of the continued type, and persists in keeping these excretory avenues closed until subsequent to the breaking out of the exanthem. It frequently happens that Aconite will not promote diaphoresis in case of a child coming down with scarlatina, or with rubeola, until this period has passed. Hence the practical inference that we should prescribe something which has a specific relation to the eruption, and which, by hastening its appearance upon the surface, may relieve the febrile condition indirectly. Belladonna may be given in the early stage of scarlet fever, or Pulsatilla in measles, as an indirect febrifuge. If, however, the attack is very mild, the general disturbance less profound, or the type of either is non-malignant, we may find the Aconite of much service.

Now these remarks apply equally to the treatment of the febrile stage of diphtheria. If the type of the epidemic is not a dangerous one, the fever not too adynamic, the throat lesion not too extensive and profound, we may rely upon Aconite alone to restore the natural moisture, and reduce the heat of the skin, the acceleration of the pulse and respiration, and the general disorder, which symptoms are more decidedly characteristic of the milder than of the more severe form of the diphtheria. But, on the other hand, where both the local and general symptoms indicate a grave attack, you will certainly accomplish the greatest good from the onset of the disease by the use of means which are more especially addressed to their relief, without wasting time in giving Aconite as a mere febrifuge, or as designed to allay the inflammatory symptoms present.

Belladonna.—Under these circumstances, if there is a marked congestion of the faucial mucous membrane, with swollen tonsils, headache, flushed face, intolerance of light and sound, and nervous irritability generally, Belladonna is certainly indicated. If the eruption resembles that of scarlatina, and the pupils are widely dilated at intervals, with active delirium, you would give this remedy, either in alternation with another, or alone.

Gelseminum would be called for in case of local tingling of parts during the fever, and a species of incipient paralysis or anæsthesia of the sensory filaments on the surface of the body, a quick pulse, hot, dry skin, and defective or impaired vision, in which objects appear a long way off (presbyopia), the patient sees double, or objects are inverted, and in those epidemics especially where miasmatic causes have modified the type of the fever—given it the intermittent or remittent characteristics. Belladonna seems more appropriate to hyperæsthesia, or a super-sensitiveness of the skin, and Gelseminum to a lack of its proper sensibility in this as in other fevers.

Rhus Toxicodendron.—If the type of the fever is decidedly adynamic, with a dry, brownish coating of the tongue and other buccal and general symptoms characteristic of a typhoid tendency, as a low, muttering delirium, oppressed breathing, a weak and irregular pulse, and especially if the throat presents, suddenly, an erysipelatous appearance, the Rhus Toxicodendron may be given. A predisposition to rheumatism on the part of the patient would lead you to prefer the same remedy.

Baptisia Tinctoria appears best adapted to the relief of low febrile states, which are marked by an excessive destruction and waste of the epithelial tissues. When flakes peel off from the surface of the oral, the alimentary, or the respiratory mucous membranes, indicative of extreme derangement in their nutritive processes, with typhoid symptoms, you may prescribe this remedy with the best results. It is also indicated in case of oppressed breathing, as from suffocation, because of pulmonary congestion. Rising in bed does not relieve this symptom; the patient must go to the window for fresh air.

Bryonia Alba may serve to relieve the gastric uneasiness. It is indicated by a bilious-looking tongue, with qualmishness, aversion to cold water, with headache, and a constipated condition of the bowels. Also, if with the fever there is a deep-seated cough, which is due to slight pulmonary engorgement, with a slow and torpid pulse, and a species of cerebral paralysis, such as we sometimes meet with in advanced stages of typhoid fever. The conditions indicating its employment are very similar to those for Rhus Tox. and Baptisia in typhoid fever.

For the Cerebral Disorder.—A few doses of Phosphorus may be of service in quieting a greatly increased activity of the brain and mental functions. The indication for this remedy would be more marked in case the respiratory mucous surfaces should feel raw and denuded, or the lungs impervious to air, with a short, hacking cough, as in the second stage of pneumonia.

Belladonna, for a super-excitation of the nerves of special sense, photophobia, objects floating before the eyes, as bright or dark spots, a thin gauze, or in incipient amaurosis, in which, from excessive dilation of the pupil, the patient cannot see distinctly.

Opium, for stupor, coma, indifference to surrounding objects or circumstances, in the later stages of diphtheria, as where the swelling of the glands of the neck embarrasses the free circulation through the vessels to the head in scarlatina maligna.

Conium-Maculatum will sometimes produce the most happy results in soporose conditions of the brain in diphtheria, especially in those cases in which, from the blue, cyanotic appearance of the skin, we infer a torpidity of circulation in the venous capillaries.

For the Mouth and Throat Symptoms.—Mercurius, in one or another of its forms, is frequently prescribed in anginose disorders. Its efficacy in certain mouth and throat affections, which are not pseudo-membranous, is well established. But the power which this agent has to produce a membranous formation in lieu of the proper epithelial structure, is not so generally understood or appreciated. Upon this subject, M. Laboulbène* says:

"The false membranes which accompany mercurial stomatitis are whitish or greyish, often thick, with shred-like borders, adherent or free, but of a marked consistence when they are attached. The mucous membrane was considerably swollen, greyish, at one time intact, again excoriated, or even ulcerated. I have not seen any very distinct sphacelus, but instead thereof a superficial ulceration, with margins more or less elevated and livid, or with a reddish, narrow border. * * * * * The false membranes appear to be true products of exudation, at least in the case which I have examined, and not sphacelated portions of buccal mucous membrane."

Mercurius furnishes the following characteristic pathogenetic symptoms, some of which are frequently present in diphtheria:†

"Painful swelling of the salivary glands; greyish ulcers on the inner surface of the lips, cheeks, gums, tongue and palate; fungous swelling of the mucous membrane of the mouth; intolerable foulness of the breath; swelling of the tongue, which

* *Loc. cit.*, p. 136.
† Hahnemann, Mat. Med. Pura, Vol. III.

is covered with a whitish, thick, tenacious coat, that is detached in shape of little skins; ulceration of the tonsils; phlegmonous angina, with lancing pain that extends to the ear, and becomes worse at night; accumulation of tenacious saliva in the mouth; complete loss of speech and voice; stitching pain in the tonsils when swallowing, and soreness which frequently extends to the ears, or to the parotid, submaxillary and cervical glands."

Upon such a basis for its therapeutical employment, there is no question but the Mercurius vivus, the M. dulcis, or the M. solubilis, may be sufficiently appropriate to the milder form of diphtheritic exudation. Many physicians give one of these in alternation with Belladonna, or some other remedy, to the exclusion of the Mercurius-jodatus; but the clinical experience of the profession does not appear to sanction their reliability in the more aggravated type of diphtheria, where the deposit is well organized and extensive. Under these latter circumstances, another preparation of Mercurius, formed by the union of this agent and Iodine, in equal parts, the M. Proto-jodatus, or of one of Mercurius to two of Iodine—M. Bi-jodatus, is generally preferred.

Iodine, given in poisonous doses, produces the following symptoms, which prove it an analogue of the specific diphtheritic virus:

"Apthæ in the mouth, with ptyalism; smarting and sensation as of pulling in the tonsils; glandular indurations; putrid smell from the mouth; troublesome dryness of the tongue; tonguo thickly coated; swelling and elongation of the uvula; ulceration in the mouth; constrictive sensation in the fauces; tormenting constriction in the throat; feeling of fulness in the throat; lacerating in the throat, above the larynx; disagreeable scraping in the fauces, with copious secretion of saliva; burning in the fauces; inflammation and ulcers of the œsophagus."*

Iodine appears, however, to be a less reliable remedy in diphtheria, when given singly, than when combined with other substances, as in Spongia, or in the Mercurius-jodatus.

* Jahr's New Manual, by Dr. Hull (Symptomatology) p. 542.

Excepting in the form of inhalation in those cases which have developed into diphtheritic croup, I am not aware that it has been much employed as a single remedy in this disease.

Mercurius-Jodatus.—The late Dr. Geo. W. Cook, of New-York, introduced this remedy to the especial notice of the profession in 1840. A perusal of the symptoms produced by it, and published by him at a later period,* will satisfy you that this compound has a therapeutical range which comprises many of the virtues of both the Mercurius and the Iodine. I select a few of these:

"Dry lips; tongue dry, and deeply chapped in the centre, deeply coated, whitish, ash-colored, velvety, deep yellow or brown; ulcers scattered along the margin of the tongue, with red edges, and an ashy-grey centre; the edge of the tongue shows the points of the teeth, where it rested against them; the buccal and submaxillary glands are enlarged, inflamed, painful, throbbing, or hard, painless and hypertrophied; parotids and tonsils are in a similar condition, and there is an abundant flow of tough saliva, with cough and expectoration of yellow mucus, or transparent, frothy mucus, with an occasional heavy flake in the centre. The uvula, tonsils, and isthmus-faucium, are inflamed; the mucous membrane of the posterior nares and pharynx is changed from its normal red hue to a deep scarlet, or even purple, as the inflammation advances in severity; passing to the chronic form, the inflammation appears more in patches, of an irregular circumscribed form, growing paler toward their circumference, until it is blended in the color of the surrounding membrane into which it merges; these patches exude a tough, white or yellowish mucus; where their inflammatory process progresses rapidly, the membrane is smooth, shining, tense, glossy and dry, and the capillaries become distinctly visible from their enlargement. The function of the mucous follicles of the entire cavity, including those at the root of the epiglottis, is so disordered as to cause them to yield an opaque, viscid and tough substance, which is some times expectorated with difficulty. The surface of the mucous membrane is raw, the epithelium being entirely destroyed."

Here, gentlemen, is the chart for the constitutional use of this invaluable remedy in the local throat affection of diph-

* Jahr's New Manual, 1851, p. 653.

theria. You will remark its evident appropriateness to those pseudo-membranous diseases of mucous tissues which involve the nutritive integrity of their epithelial covering; and also to swelling and induration of the glands in and adjacent to the mouth and fauces. From this analysis of its sphere of operation, and from the accumulated experience of the profession in its employment, we are enabled to deduce the following general rules for its therapeutical use:

1. The M.-jodatus is most appropriate to those examples and epidemics of diphtheria in which the deposit is located in or upon the mouth, the tongue, the tonsils, the uvula, the vellum palati, the pharynx, or some portion of the alimentary tract.

2. To those cases in which the function of the mucous follicles is so deranged as to produce, in considerable quantity, the tough and viscid secretion of which we have spoken.

3. The deposit should be of limited extent, of feeble organization, transparent, pellicular, albuminous, and easily detached.

4. To those cases in which there is but a feeble effort at a re-organization of false membrane, when it has been removed, or has dropped off spontaneously; and

5. To such examples of diphtheria as are characterized by marked disorder of one portion or another of the alimentary system.

I believe there are other remedies which promise better results in case the lesion has invaded any part of the respiratory tract. The reason for this is to be found in the varying anatomy and physiological function of the two kinds of epithelial surface. In the mouth, the throat and œsophagus, excepting only the respiratory compartment of the pharynx, the mucous membrane is coated with squamous epithelial cells. The epithelium upon the infra-diaphragmatic surfaces is of the columnar or cylindrical variety. That which coats the respiratory mucous membrane is of the ciliated order, and for aught we know, these latter may be, and probably are charged with a function and susceptibilities as different from those of the former as are their anatomical configuration. Indeed, it is a matter of common observation that, when the pseudo-membrane has formed upon any portion of the respiratory surfaces, it is always more firmly organized. This is the chief reason why we dread to have it encroach upon the glottis, the larynx, or the trachea. Those who have seen much of the diphtheria, have recognized that, even in the nasal cavities, which properly belong to the respiratory tract, the pseudo-membrane differs in firmness of texture and tenacity from that found upon the squamous surfaces of the throat proper. It would appear, therefore, that this pathological peculiarity should have weight in the selection of the proper remedy. I beg you will not overlook its significance.

My own preference is decidedly in favor of the Proto-iodide, as a more reliable and satisfactory remedy in diphtheria than the Bin-iodide. In this it conforms with that of Dr. Helmuth,* who says: "I have carefully noticed the action of this remedial agent in contradistinction to the *Bin-iodide*, and must bear testimony to its more speedy and more effectual action." The two equivalents of Iodine in the latter, in my own professional experience, have sometimes appeared to prove too irritating to the fauces and the posterior nares, thus defeating the very design of the prescription.

In severe cases where the M.-jodatus is indicated, and you give it singly, a grain, or one grain and a half, of the second or third tritruation, may be repeated once in one or two hours. It is my custom, when I desire to make a decided impression, to repeat the dose hourly for three hours, and then to protract the interval somewhat. It may be given in this low form—the trituration being always preferred—in alternation with Belladonna, Cantharis, Arsenicum, or almost any of the more ordinary remedies, without the least interference with their curative action.

Cantharis.—Numerous French authorities, among whom are Guibourt, Gerdy, Bouillaud, Bretonneau, and Laboul-

* *Loc. cit.*, p. 88.

bène have spoken of the production of false-membrane resulting from the action of the Cantharides. Indeed, there are few among the elder practioners of medicine who have not witnessed organized exudations upon the skin after being denuded of its cuticle by a blister. Bretonneau concludes the membrane produced by Cantharides is identical with that of diphtheria.

This celebrated authority* reports the results of an experiment which we are constrained to quote:

"A ball of the ethereal extract of the powder of cantharides, having scarcely the volume of a hemp-seed, dissolved in a small spoonful of olive oil, was administered to a goat. There was fatal poisoning, and the body was examined. There were no traces of the coriaceous epithelium which covers the tongue, the œsophagus, and the first stomach; but the enormous concrete exudation which occupied its place exhibited the most exact model of the surfaces, from which the exudation was being detached in prodigious quantity."

Laboulbène† says:

"The false membrane produced by the active principle of the cantharides bears a close resemblance to that of diphtheria. I have frequently observed upon my own person the effect of the oil of cantharides placed upon the mucous membrane on the inner surface of the lips. * * * * * * In May, 1852, while studying the action of the oil of cantharides employed as a rapid blistering agent, I placed a drop of this oil upon the inner or buccal surface of my lower lip. The drop was placed on a little roll of oiled linen, of four millimètres in diameter; the lip was depressed and kept in contact with the oiled linen by means of a glass plate.

"Pain resulted as soon as the application was made upon the mucous membrane, previously well dried. The pain became very severe, and through the glass I saw the decidedly injected condition of the vessels, around the linen. After some minutes I substituted for the glass plate a very small and convex watch-glass. The pain had diminished; I thought the action of the oil of cantharides had taken place.

"The epithelium was raised and I found a bulla resembling those of pemphigus; the pain was very sharp around this

* Memoirs on Diphtheria, (New Sydenham Society,) London, 1859, p. 186.

† *Loc. cit.*, p. 160.

bulla, but less so than one would have supposed after the pain and the congestion in the commencement of the process.

"The liquid coating was rapidly solidified; after having waited for twenty minutes, I removed it in order to examine it. It was of a whitish color, and presented, upon microscopical examination, a veined structure, formed of an amorphous substance, enclosing fibrillæ crossed by parallel fibres, molecular granulations, and a greyish matter of a granular form. In scraping away the plastic production, I detached some epithelial scales which were from the coating of epithelium raised by the serous effusion.

"Four hours later, I removed the deposit which had reproduced itself and which had a marked thickness. Examined upon its under surface, there was seen, with the foregoing elements, pus-globules and manifest granular cells.

"In the evening the exudative coating was re-produced. It remained the next day without having changed its elementary composition. The day following, the plastic deposit had diminished in thickness; it disappeared by a species of wearing away; the surrounding redness became extinguished, and the surface included some epithelial cells. The following days the exuded product was gone; there remained only a vascular redness, which disappeared slowly."

Dr. Sanderson* injected into the air-passages of several dogs, small quantities of a solution of Cantharides in olive oil, and examined the consequent alterations of the mucous membrane after various periods. In two hours the mucous surface of the larynx was scattered over with patches, the structure was covered with a gelatinous coating of tolerably firm concretion, differing from that of diphtheria only in its greater transparency. This concretion, he reports, possessed a structure identical with that of the early stage of diphtheria.

If, therefore, you are called upon to treat cases of diphtheria in which the oral or faucial mucous membrane is dotted here and there with more or less extended patches of the pseudo-membrane, which deposit is elevated and filled beneath with serum, as in a blister, or the membrane is thin and pellicular, feebly organized, transparent, and has been rapidly formed upon a surface more or less erythematous, you should

* British and Foreign Med. Chir. Rev., Jan., 1860, pp. 181–9.

prescribe the Cantharis as a constitutional remedy. These indications will be strengthened by such symptoms as the following: Considerable derangement in the urinary organs, too copious or difficult urination, strangury, the passage of urine containing membranous shreds, which in the field of the microscope, and sometimes by the naked eye, are recognized as other than exfoliated tubal casts. Extreme prostration, sinking, death-like turns, with sympathetic derangement of the excretory function of the skin, and an irritable looking rash upon its surface, or directly beneath the epidermis, are symptoms which, in addition to those already enumerated, appear to demand the employment of the Cantharis.

It is my habit to put ten drops of the second attenuation of this remedy into half a glass of cold water, and order a tea-spoonful thereof every one to three hours for a child under two years. If the patient is older than this, I recommend two tea-spoonfuls, to be taken at longer or shorter intervals, according to the urgency of the symptoms.

Bi-chromate of Potassa.—The second volume of the British Journal of Homœopathy contains an excellent and finely illustrated article upon the toxical and pathological effects of this agent on the epithelial coat of the various mucous membranes. I recommend you to study it carefully, in order to arrive at a true conception of its curative sphere of action. By such a process, you will doubtless reach conclusions somewhat akin to the following, which, *en passant*, are based upon the extended experience of some of the best physicians in the North-West:

1. This remedy seems especially appropriate to pseudo-membranous lesions of a diphtheritic nature affecting the respiratory mucous surfaces, as the nares, the superior portion of the pharynx, the larynx, the trachea, and the bronchial tubes, even down to their ultimate ramifications.

2. Where the deposit is of firmer texture, more apt to be developed into casts which are cartillaginous, or pearly in appearance, elastic, fibrinous, and more securely attached to the subjacent integument.

3. It is indicated in all those cases where a transfer of the local disorder to the larynx or trachea impends, as shown by soreness of the larynx when pressed upon from before backwards, aphonia, croupy inspiration or cough, and a desire on the part of the patient to lie with the head thrown far backwards, in order to throw open the glottis.

4. It may also be given with excellent results in case the tonsils are almost or quite enveloped by a thick and well-organized deposit, and in which at the same time the patient has an almost incessant cough.

5. Also where, with the foregoing symptoms, there is an evident tendency to ulceration and deposit upon remote mucous membranes, as for example those of the uterine system. In my own experience, the Bi-chromate is almost a specific to diphtheritic formations upon the free uterine, and to those found upon the respiratory epithelial surfaces.

6. Since in all these cases the putrid symptoms are less marked than in the pharyngeal and alimentary diphtheria, you should take the hint to cease the employment of the Bi-chromate when these symptoms ensue. The Iodide of Arsenic, Nitric Acid, or Carbo Vegetabilis, are much more decidedly indicated for the relief of such a condition.

The Bi-chromate of Potassa may be given in the second or third decimal trituration, and repeated every one to three or four hours. Like the Merc-jodatus its action does not appear to be neutralized by alternating it with any of the more ordinary remedies.

Tartar Emetic seems also possessed of a specific relation to the respiratory mucous surfaces. It may not be known to you that its constitutional action will produce a pseudo-membrane upon the buccal, the laryngeal and tracheal mucous surfaces. The work of M. Laboulbène, which I have in my hand, is embellished with a beautifully colored lithograph of this pathological product, which you may examine at the close of the lecture.

In the text of this author, at page 132, I read: "The false

membranes produced by Tartar Emetic in the cavity of the mouth, and principally upon the tongue, have the form of irregularly rounded patches, whitish or greyish in color, somewhat thick, of a marked consistence and firmly adherent. In the œsophagus, they are small, delicate, pale, and easily detached from the subjacent tissue.

"Beneath the pseudo-membrane, the lingual mucous structure is excoriated, ecchymosed, wrinkled, and forms an elevated margin around the plastic deposit, which is red and somewhat extended. The œsophageal mucous membrane is ulcerated, the borders of this ulceration are not elevated, but enclosed by a red circle, the base being softened and greyish, and, at some points, ecchymosed."

The indications which, in my own experience, more frequently require this remedy in diphtheria, are, sudden swelling of the cervical glands and tonsils, occurring in scrofulous children, who are predisposed to catarrhal or asthmatic affections; occlusion of the larynx or lower respiratory channels, by excess of mucus, or of a feebly organized plasma, with cough, dysphagia, difficulty of breathing, gasping (which compels the patient to sit upright, or to seek the open air); inclination to retching and vomiting, obstinate vomiting of a tenacious mucus, without any considerable thirst; small circular patches, like small-pox pustules, in and upon the mouth and tongue; and also for evidences of closure of the pulmonary air-vesicles by solidification of effused serum (hepatization). It will sometimes serve a good purpose by promoting diaphoresis, and, in exceptional cases, will drive out the eruption, to the great relief of internal mucous surfaces.

I recommend you not to overlook the claims of this remedy in certain forms and varieties of the diphtheritic lesion. In particular, it seems applicable to many cases of diphtheria, in which the abnormal throat and chest symptoms derive their chief characteristics from a prevalent influenza, or from an inherent predisposition on the part of the patient to catarrhal disorders of the respiratory mucous membrane. I usually prescribe it in the second or third decimal trituration, of which two grains may be dissolved in half a glass of water, and a teaspoonful administered every one to three or four hours.

Rhus Toxicodendron is very serviceable as a constitutional remedy in diphtheria in cases marked by considerable adynamia, with a proneness to that variety of capillary engorgement and inflammation of mucous and cutaneous structures which is denominated "erysipelatous." If the throat is congested, of a dark red, or of a cranberry color, with considerable elevation of the injected portions, the swelling coming up suddenly, as it sometimes does in genuine erysipelas, or in the species of eruption vulgarly called "hives," you may rely upon the appropriateness of the remedy. Where the deposit has changed its color, and become brownish, or even of a darker hue, and a little bloody, and the tongue and teeth, in the later stages, appear as in typhoid fever, with a kind of stupor without rest, it may be of essential service.

The Iodide of Arsenic is best adapted to the putrid symptoms, and those alimentary disturbances which follow the disease. It does not appear to be so appropriate to the lesion in and about the throat, in the earlier stages, as some of the remedies already enumerated. When, however, the oral and faucial mucous membranes have become dry and fissured, flaky and offensive; when evidences of putrefactive decomposition are manifest in the breath, from the presence of this post-organic matter, retained in contact with the saliva and other fluids, are present, and there is every reason to fear the ill cosequences from its resorption, you may prescribe this agent with beneficial results.

Every one familiar with the curative sphere of the Arsenicum recognizes its appropriateness to symptoms which result from the absorption of organic poisons. Those physicians who practice in miasmatic districts, and especially if beside bodies of water, or in heavily timbered bottom-lands, make this a chief indication for its employment in many diseases. You are aware of the close similarity of action between the intangible diphtheritic virus and the Iodine, in so far as resulting local lesions of the mucous membranes are concerned. This knowledge, in absence of a thorough and reliable proving of the Ars.-jodatus, leads us to infer its clinical value just here.

Baptisia-Tinctoria is known to have occasioned sore mouth with salivation; also white looking ulcers upon the tongue and fauces. Symptoms which indicate it, as shown under the head of Fever, may find a confirmation in this characteristic pathological lesion. Dr. E. M. Hale places great reliance upon it as a remedy for the oral and anginose symptoms in diphtheria. Dr. D. W. Rogers, of Quincy, Mich., recommends the Baptisia internally in malignant, putrid cases, with purplish ecchymosed spots on the body or extremities of the size of a quarter of a dollar or less. He thinks it should be prescribed thus in a low attenuation, or even in the mother tincture, frequently repeated.

Nitric Acid.—My friend Dr. J. P. Dake, of Pittsburg, prefers this remedy in case "the peculiar membrane is present, the ulcers are persistent, or the elevated patches appear." He recommends this acid in alternation with Capsicum and Belladonna. In the apthous form of the disease he prescribes Borax in the second trituration, with one of the two last-named remedies. Dr. Dake* says:

"I recommend *Nitric Acid*, than which there is no remedy more capable of meeting the disease, without and within, locally and constitutionally. It not only touches the patchwork, but also follows on through every avenue traversed by the destroyer—quickening the powers of gland, mucous membrane, and stomach, for its expulsion, the repair of tissue and the support of life."

Apis Mellifica is most appropriate where the roof of the mouth is swollen, œdematous, and the superior pharynx and faucial cavity present a whitish, glossy, tense condition, with fever and burning pains in these parts. Each effort to swallow occasions pain, which extends into the ear. The palate is so swollen as not to be flexible, and the patient complains of a sensation as of a thousand little needles sticking into it. If the inflammation resembles phlegmonous erysipelas, or the eruption upon the skin is accompanied by an intol-

* North American Journal of Homœopathy, Vol. X, p. 433.

erable itching, as in urticaria, the indication for this remedy is a very decided one.

B a r y t a C a r b o n i c a.—In those examples, in the early stage of which it is difficult to tell if the case will prove to be one of diphtheria, or of tonsilitis, in which the tonsils and pharyngeal mucous membrane present a reddish, glossy appearance, there is free spitting of mucus, and in which, at first thought, the Mercurius-jodatus would seem to be indicated, Dr. R. B. Clarke prescribes, of the Carbonate of Baryta, in the first to the third decimal trituration, a grain, dry upon the tongue, repeated once in three to six hours. Its sphere of action appears to lie between Belladonna and Mercurius, or Nitric Acid, since it is adapted at once to the relief of the congestion, and of a too copious secretion from the oral and pharyngeal mucous surfaces.

B e l l a d o n n a.—This remedy is singularly beneficial in most cases of diphtheria. When the lining membrane of the throat, the buccal cavity, and neighboring glands, are congested, and the functional activity of the epithelial cells greatly increased, because of the undue afflux of blood, the Belladonna is invaluable. Redness and swelling of the tonsils, and dryness of the fauces, as in simple angina, with other characteristic symptoms, will be promptly relieved by it. A majority of practitioners employ it in every case of the disease. It is mostly given in alternation with one or another of the foregoing remedies. A glance at its pathogenesy, and a single good result of its prescription in conformity therewith will satisfy you of its wonderful virtues in relieving these prominent and distressing symptoms.

For the Odor of the Breath.—The internal employment of A r s e n i c u m A l b u m, C h i n a, the N i t r i c, M u r i a t i c, and S u l p h u r i c A c i d s, of some preparation of M e r c u r i u s, B a p t i s i a - T i n c t., or of small doses of a weak solution of C h l o r a t e o f P o t a s s a, or even of N a t r u m M u r i a t i c u m,—common table-salt, are recommended for this peculiar symptom.

For the Coryza.—The Mercurius-jodatus will, in most cases, be sufficient to remedy this condition, unless, indeed, there be a firmly organized deposit within the nostril, with pseudo-membraneous exudation upon the inferior portions of the respiratory mucous membrane. In this event, you will witness the most prompt and satisfactory results from the use of the Bi-chromate of Potassa.

For the Gastric and Alimentary Disorder.—Dr. G. W. Bowen, of Fort Wayne, Ind., places more reliance upon Nux Vomica than upon any other remedy for the relief of the alimentary disorder incident to diphtheria. In some cases, Bryonia Alba effects very great relief, and I have a few times prescribed Opium in those cases in which the nervous centres were evidently paralyzed and the nutritive system suffered indirectly, the symptoms being those of torpidity of function, lack of proper peristaltic activity in the stomach and other portions of the intestinal tract, and constipation. The Veratrum Album, and again Phosphoric Acid and Arsenicum may be of service. Superior to these, however, I am constrained to place the Merc.-jodatus, which appears possessed of reliable properties for the relief of diarrhœic states, especially those which so frequently accompany, or supervene the true diphtheria. This remedy, for this condition, is of more value than any other.

Nitric Acid will meet the indications which ordinarily call for its employment. It seems so *en rapport* with the general condition upon which this symptom depends as frequently to render it very reliable.

Arsenicum-jodatus is appropriate to alimentary disorders resulting from a depraved and putrid condition of the blood and solids. Where the symptoms are referable to the resorption of organic matters, in the later stages of malignant diphtheria, you will find it preferable to the Arsenicum Album.

Mercurius-jodatus will answer an excellent purpose where, in addition to pathogenetic symptoms, there is considerable derangement of the function of the liver and of the lower bowels. Where the stools are bilious-looking, sometimes clay-colored, and very offensive, indicating a scanty supply of bile to the intestine, or black and tarry, with or without tenesmus, you may prescribe it with excellent results. This remedy, indeed, like the two last-named, appears to have such a specific relation to the diphtheritic poison as to antidote its entire action.

Cantharis is serviceable in those occasional cases which are accompanied by intestinal colic, with almost constant tenesmus of the rectum.

For the Eruption.—Belladonna is the remedy in case the eruption is bright, scarlet, diffuse, accompanied by a pungent heat of the skin, resembling scarlatina.

Rhus Toxicodendron, if it is dark, elevated into ridges or welts, or has an erysipelatous appearance.

Bryonia Alb., when it resembles measles, is easily repelled from the surface by exposure to the air, or is accompanied by a catarrhal cough, with more or less of gastric disorder.

Nitric Acid, for an eruption which dark in color, mottled in appearance, or hæmorrhagic and purpuric in character, occurring only in the more malignant cases.

Arsenicum-jodatus meets nearly the same indications. I am disposed to recommend this remedy for the cure of the eruption in those cases of cerebro-spinal meningitis which are known as "spotted fever," and which, I have no question, are of a diphtheritic nature. The Ars.-jodatus corresponds not only to the eruptive or petechial symptoms, but also to the more profound lesions of the cerebro-spinal meninges. It might be given with Belladonna, Gelseminum, or some other remedy.

Cantharis and Rhus Toxicodendron are indicated when the eruption is vesicular, and there are bullæ resembling those of pemphigus, or when it resembles vesicular erysipelas, appears suddenly, and as suddenly declines.

For the Urinary Symptoms.—Aconite will sometimes promote a free discharge of urine where the heat and excess of fever, have suppressed it. Physicians often prescribe it for its dipaphoretic effect, and are led to marvel how it can produce such excellent results,—how it can relieve the fever without copious sweating, when it has simply carried off the critical fluid by the kidneys. You should not forget the close functional sympathy between the skin and the kidneys.

Merc.-jodatus is sometimes a good remedy in case of suppression of urine in diphtheria.

Cantharis is invaluable in case of retention with strangury, or tenesmus of the bladder, shown by repeated, almost ineffectual, and very painful attempts at micturition. If there are shreds of membrane, which, in the field of the microscope, appear to be other than tubal casts, true diphtheritic productions exfoliated from the renal mucous membrane, there is no remedy to compare with this. Laboulbène, in the work to which I have already referred, gives a detailed description of the formation of a pathological membrane in the kidneys from poisoning with Cantharides.

Ammonia-acet.—A weak solution of this salt in water is recommended as a certain means of relief in case of retention of the urine.

Diluent Drinks.—Slippery Elm water, Gum Arabic water, or either of the ordinary bland, demulcent drinks, taken in considerable quantities, may serve to relieve this symptom, by "washing out the kidneys," as the old women say.

Merc.-corrosivus, Phosphoric Acid, Arsenicum Alb., are our most reliable remedies in albuminuria. In most cases of diphtheritic albuminuria, I believe the former to be preferable. You should anticipate this symptom, and thus strive to prevent relapses among your patients. Physicians frequently treat diphtheria for a few days, until the acute symptoms have subsided, and then dismiss themselves any further professional care, with instructions to the nurse or parent not to let the little fellow take cold. In a week or ten days, the patient is ill again, and the symptoms, among which is albuminuria, are more grave than at first. Such relapses may possibly be prevented by a timely use of one of the foregoing remedies.

Colchicum is the most promising remedy for uræmic poisoning. There is little question, however, but the Merc.-jodatus, the Nitric Acid, Cantharis, or Ars.-jodatus, might be of service in many cases. You should strive to remove this symptom before the organic lesion of the kidney is become too profound.

For the Sudden and Extreme Debility.—The treatment for this characteristic symptom is mostly hygienic.

China will exert a wonderful influence for the relief of the marked prostration in diphtheria, the "sinking spells," especially if they recur at a given time, and for the feeling as if one had been exhausted by a profuse diarrhœa, or other debilitating discharge. It should be given in a low attenuation, and at brief intervals.

Cantharis.—In illustration of the remarkable similarity between the effects of this agent and the poison of diphtheria,—an item which may be of essential service to you as practitioners, I quote from Bretonneau again: *

"In both cases, there was the same coldness, yielding to no process of warming, even in the midst of summer; the same absolute adynamia, which cannot be compared to any other adynamia, or rather it is a complete extinction of muscular power; no other movements remain, except those of the heart or of the respiration, and even these movements are so slow that the pulse falls to fifty, thirty, twenty, five pulsations in the minute, then to only one in two minutes. There is a corresponding decrease in the expiratory movements, and at last extinction of life, with this remarkable difference, that the

* *Loc. cit.*, pp. 186–7.

death caused by the Egyptian (diphtheritic) poison is *real*. * * * * After the poison of Cantharides, death is only apparent before becoming real. We have twice, and even thrice, seen this fictitious death repeated; on which occasions, this apparent death so closely resembled real death, that the instinct of the great blue fly was deceived by it. A swarm of these flies, which deposit their larvæ on meat when it is beginning to turn, covered the commissures of the eyelids, the lips, and the apertures of the nostrils, with a thick and rounded layer of these heaped-up larvæ.

"Each of these successive fits of lethargy was generally prolonged more than twenty minutes, without our being able to perceive any indication of life, or to excite even a dubious movement of the heart during the continuance of this apparent death, when, to our great astonishment, we saw a kind of resurrection, at first slow, then rapid, so that the animals became able to stand and walk; subsequently, there was a more prolonged relapse, and finally complete extinction of life."

I am quite confident the profession in general are not aware of the remarkable virtues of Cantharis in relieving this peculiar prostration common to diphtheria. Let me, therefore, commend you not to overlook its claims as an important and most promising remedy for this symptom.

For the Hæmorrhage.—For this concomitant of diphtheria, in one or another of its forms, you may use, internally, the Hamamelis Virg., Nitric Acid, Sulphuric Acid, China, Erechthites Hier. (?) and Arsenicum Album.

II.—LOCAL TREATMENT.

First, of the avulsion, or forcible removal of the pseudomembranous deposit. Some physicians have a strange propensity to tear away the false membrane. They will tell you it is necessary to detach it forcibly, and recommend its removal from the throats of both old and young, under the plea that it is a foreign body, and that its presence interferes with the direct application of local agents to the sub-mucous structure. Dr. Condie says: *

"The removal of the membraniform deposit from the fauces, or the prevention of its accumulation and extension is always to be attended to. It is a measure calculated to give great relief to the patient, and will concur with the general treatment in rendering his recovery more prompt and certain."

Other eminent authorities are opposed to such a proceeding. Thus, Dr. Wade remarks: †

"The faucial exudation of diphtheria is to be considered as the local manifestation of a general disease. Interference with it will not prevent its reproduction, nor will it prevent laryngeal complication, nor will it prevent the supervention of grave constitutional disorder. It is exceedingly irksome to young patients. We are justified in interfering with the throat exudation when there is excessive fœtor, or when it is so copious as to interfere with respiration or deglutition, not otherwise."

Dr. Ormerod‡ is of opinion that—

"As a rule, nothing is gained by detaching this deposit, for it will speedily be re-produced, and the operation causes much distress, if not actual pain, to the patient; and in estimating the probable benefit from such interference, we must remember that, besides the exudation which we see, and can reach, there is probably much that we can neither see nor reach, and must perforce leave alone; though, on the whole, I believe that this typical exudation is more marked on the parts of the soft palate which are in sight than anywhere else, the plastic exudations on the interior of the larynx and bronchii only excepted."

There are several reasons why this avulsion of the diphtheritic membrane should not be practiced It frightens the child, and causes him pain. The plastic deposit is not only re-organized, but more firmly so than at first, thus throwing an obstacle in the way of an early return of the healthy nutrition and function. If left alone, it will be spontaneously detached, and under these circumstances is seldom re-formed

* Proceedings of Phila. Co. Med. Society, 1862.
† London Lancet for Nov. 1862, p. 269.
‡ Notes on Diphtheria, *op. citat.* 165.

upon the same surface. It increases the liability to an extension of the lesion to more vital parts, and exhausts the patient's strength by causing an unnecessary drain of albuminous plasma.

A tea-spoonful of the liquor sanguinis exuded thus abnormally, will sometimes debilitate a patient almost as much as a copious blood-letting.

Various experiments have been made with a view to test the effect of chemical reagents upon the diphtheritic false membrane. Among them the most interesting are those of M. Laboulbène,* who sums up his observations as follows:

" *Cold Water* does not act at first upon the diphtheritic false membrane; it is but slowly and after several days that this product becomes disintegrated, but without being dissolved;†

" *Boiling water* dissolves a small portion of it, but renders the remainder of the mass opaque, condensed, and hardened;

" *Alcohol* shrivels and hardens the false membranes; separating their fatty elements;

" *Sulphuric Acid*, when dilute, dries up and shrivels the false membranes, turning them of a brownish color;

" *Nitric Acid* has an analogous effect, turning them yellowish; after a long time the plastic product is reduced to clots or lumps by its action;

" *Chlorohydric Acid*, especially in the concentrated form, has a more solvent action than that of the preceding acids, but less so than the acetic acid. Employed cold, the spread of this acid sometimes gives the paste a violet or greenish tint; with heat, the tint is violet;

" *Acetic Acid* causes the membranes to swell, renders them more pale in hue, and in time dissolves them;

" *Chromic Acid*, in a very dilute form, swells and stiffens them in a remarkable manner;

" The *Tincture of Iodine* turns them yellow, reddish, and renders them very tough;

---

* *Recherches Cliniques et Anatomiques sur les affections: Pseudo-Membraneuses*, etc., Par A. Laboulbene, Paris, 1861, p. 87.

† M. Isambert thinks that *oxygenated water*, which is instantly decomposed in the presence of fibrin, would serve to distinguish solidified albumen. (*Archiv. gen. de med.*, T. IX, p. 328.) This re-action is not of easy applicability in the chemical diagnosis of pseudo-membranous formations.

" A solution of *Nitrate of Silver* renders the false membranes more pale, then contracts and shrivels them, but does not dissolve them. The color afterwards becomes of a brownish hue;

" Solutions of *Potassa*, of *Soda*, and of *Ammonia*, soften the false membranes, cause them to become gelatinous, soluble like starch; they are fluid and shred-like when the vessel is inverted. This effect is especially remarked in case of the ammonia;

" The solution of *sub-carbonate of these bases* has a less marked but similar effect. This action is much more rapid with the aid of heat, applied by means of a spirit-lamp;

" The *Concentrated Solution of Nitrate of Potassa* softens the false membranes and renders them quite transparent;

" A *solution of Chlorate of Potassa* causes them to become semi-transparent and dissolved at the end of twenty-four hours;

" The *solution of Chlorate of Soda* has a similar effect, but acts twice as promptly;

" The solution of *Bi-chromate of Potassa* toughens the membrane slightly, but does not render it friable;

" *Bromine-water* acts upon the false membranes so that after twelve hours they become harsh and friable; if one touches them in the solution, they are disintegrated, and fall into powder;

" The *Bromide of Potassium* has an action which is more marked; the false membranes plunged in the solution for twelve hours, become transparent, softened, diffuse; after three days they have disappeared, and there remains only some molecular granulations at the bottom of the vessel;

" *Glycerine* renders the diphtheritic pseudo-membranes transparent and puffs them up.

" The result of these various experiments establishes the essential fibrinous character of the false membrane in diphtheria."

Of the numerous topical applications recommended by the profession, the following are the more important:

Chloride of Sodium, or common salt, of which a weak solution is used as a gargle in domestic practice. In the milder cases it may sometimes be employed with great benefit, and possesses this merit, that it is always available, no matter where you shall find your patient. There is no doubt that this simple preparation is possessed of equal virtues with the Chlorinated Soda, which is extolled in diphtheria by Mr. Alford.* Some physicians recommend that cloths dipped in salt-water shall be applied around the neck in this disease, and it may be well for you sometimes to recommend them. The water holding the salt in solution should be hot or cold, as the patient may prefer.

Hydrochloric Acid.—"Of local remedies, the Hydrochloric Acid stands first in general estimation."† Bretonneau recommended to apply a mixture of one part of this acid and three parts of honey to the throat. Dr. Morgan ‡ thinks highly of the local employment of dilute Muriatic Acid in diphtheria. Dr. Helmuth§, although he does not set a very high value upon topical means, prefers a solution composed of two parts of Muriatic Acid to one of water.

Baptisia Tinctoria.—Dr. E. M. Hale places great confidence in this remedy prepared in proportion of a drachm of the strong tincture to four fluid-ounces of water. This may be used as a gargle, especially in cases characterized by an ulcerated condition of the buccal and faucial mucous membrane, with a more or less fœtid odor.

Muriated Tincture of Iron is recommended by Dr. Madden. ‖ His plan is to paint the fauces once in twelve hours with this tincture, and four times daily with Glycerine. It is most appropriate to cases complicated with erysipelas.

Iodine.—Inhalations of this substance are certainly of service where the membranous deposit has invaded the larynx and trachea, and croupy symptoms are present in a marked degree. If you have not an inhaler at hand, it is possible to extemporize one thus: Fill an ordinary tea-pot half full of boil-

* British Medical Journal of March 8th, 1859.
† N. Am. Medico-Chirurgical Review, Vol. III., p. 418.
‡ Monthly Homœopathic Review, Vol. V.
§ A Treatise on Diphtheria, etc., p. 80.
‖ British Journal of Hom., Vol. XVII., p. 232.

ing water, and then pour into it a table-spoonful of the Iodine. Close the lid and permit the vapor to escape through the spout into the air which is breathed by the patient.

Bromine may be employed in the same manner under similar indications. Inhalations of Bromine are reputed serviceable also in cases having an erysipelatous tendency. You may be aware of the fact that the wards of some of our military hospitals are fumigated with this substance, which not only prevents the spread of the erysipelas, but exerts a curative influence over the eruption itself.

Bi-chromate of Potassa.—In a few extreme cases, involving the respiratory surfaces, Dr. Lord* has employed inhalations of the second trituration of this salt with surprising results. Half a tea-cupful of hot water may be poured upon two or three grains, and the vapor inhaled.

Nitric Acid is only appropriate as a local application to those varieties of plastic deposit which are non-diphtheritic, but parasitic in their nature.

Kreosote, diluted with water, has considerable reputation as a topical agent in diphtheria. It is an excellent antiseptic, and may be indicated in case this disease occurs during dentition, or is engrafted upon a syphilitic dyscrasia.

Ammonium Causticum.—Dr. J. P. Dake† extols the inhalation of this remedy "in cases attended with great irritation of the nasal ducts, swelling or ulceration of their lining membrane, or copious, fluent coryza."

Chlorate of Potassa is an excellent antiseptic in very malignant cases. The same is true of the chlorinated water first recommended by Dr. Watson.

I might refer you to other substances which have been used as topical remedies in this disease, but it must suffice to say that the more reliable and experienced practitioners place greater confidence in the employment of a well-chosen constitu-

* Trans. Ill. Hom. Med. Association, 1862, p. 67.
† North American Journal of Homœopathy, Vol. X., p. 480.

tional treatment. In exceptional cases, you may do well to prescribe one of the local means just named. You should bear in mind, however, that the pseudo-membranous exudation in diphtheria is but the local manifestation of a general disease, the course of which can no more be changed than can the course of either of the specific fevers by local means alone.

As a rule, the local treatment of this affection cannot be too soothing and gentle. My own practice is to employ a gargle of cow's milk, diluted with an equal quantity of warm water. This may be used freely and frequently, and if the little patient will drink it, the benefit will be doubled. In case of laryngeal spasm, inhalations of steam from hot water afford great relief.

Externally, I prefer that the neck should be enveloped in raw cotton, or in flannel—something to keep it warm—especially if it be lame or stiff. Where you find a piece of salt-pork or ham already applied, it is well enough to permit it to remain. Oily substances may serve to keep the cervical integument soft and less painful. Cold water locally does not appear to answer so well in the diphtheritic sore-throat as in ordinary angina and tonsillitis. I have known it to occasion the most frightful laryngeal spasm.

III.—HYGIENIC TREATMENT.

The sick chamber should be well ventilated, the atmosphere dry, and the temperature kept at 65° to 70° F. both day and night. Avoid currents of cool air. The patient should not be permitted to leave the room. If a little child has diphtheria, even of the mildest possible type, keep it off the floor. If you have more than one ill in the same house with this disease, your best plan will be to separate them. Send one into one room and another into another, or if possible, let them occupy different houses. While lying in the same chamber, two patients with diphtheria are constantly infecting each other. Under these circumstances convalescence will be more tedious, much less certain, and relapses frequent.

It is all-important to keep the patient well supplied with nourishment. If an infant, let it nurse freely and frequently. The mother's milk will lubricate and soothe the throat, besides nourishing the child. If older, feed him well. Do not be afraid of doing mischief by recommending and insisting upon a sustaining treatment. Repudiate the old idea that "milk makes fever," and that all your patients indiscriminately should be starved in order to facilitate or ensure recovery. This is an adynamic, and not an inflammatory disorder. The nutritive processes are imperilled. If you cut off supplies, your patient will almost certainly succumb. Begin early to insist upon his taking food. I frequently order that milk be taken several times daily, and in considerable amount, throughout the whole course of the disease. Bits of ice, ice-cream, orange, orange or lemonade, will frequently be grateful, and are never objectionable when asked for.

A sense of choking or of pain upon attempting to swallow may serve to frighten away the appetite; but this obstacle should be surmounted. If your patient is very weak, give him beef-tea, eggs and milk beaten together, oyster broth, bits of oysters, a plain custard, or wine whey. The ordinary tea, toast and rice, *alias* "slops," will not suffice. If he cannot swallow, you may administer some of the most fluid and diffusible of the foregoing per rectum. He must be nourished, from the commencement, and with such an aliment as is stimulating, and most available for histogenetic purposes. Unless you comply with this physiological condition of life in the tissues, the chances are that health will never be restored in them.

Every article, as knives, forks, spoons, plates, etc., used by the patient, should be thoroughly cleaned before being used for any other purpose. Physicians are conservators as well as restorers of the public health.

IV.—SURGICAL TREATMENT.

Tracheotomy is a *dernier ressort* in diphtheria. I have no confidence in it in this disease. Diphtheria is an affection of which the local lesion is the least important part. Its erratic nature, its proneness to re-appear upon a neighboring or remote surface, argues very strongly against the promise of success by local treatment alone. If you remove the plastic deposit from the trachea by a surgical operation, a few hours later will be apt to reveal symptoms of a like formation within the larynx or the bronchii. Possibly this operation may be serviceable in croup, but not in diphtheria. Indeed, the celebrated French authorities, who so much extol this expedient, are all of them the most strenuous advocates for the identity of these two diseases, a fact which should be taken into the account in estimating the value of their tables, which seem to have been framed for the purpose of proving the utility of tracheotomy in diphtheria.

Laryngotomy.—The same objections hold with reference to this operation. Should you determine to perform either of them, however, I must refer you to surgical authorities for details.

Excision of the Tonsils.—This cruel operation is unnecessary, brutal, barbarous. There are constitutional and local means for lessening the tumefaction of these organs, which are always at hand, and should be resorted to in preference to their excision. The operation is justifiable, if at all, only in those sudden and extreme cases in which the œdematous tonsils threaten to asphyxiate the patient, and the mechanical source of suffocation must be at once removed.

Tubage of the Larynx is an operation so difficult of performance and so dangerous in its remote consequences to this organ, as to prove substantially inexpedient and unsuccessful. At the best, it would be merely palliative. The disease is systemic, and not local. We must, therefore, place our chief reliance upon therapeutical, and not upon surgical means of relief.

www.ingramcontent.com/pod-product-compliance
Lightning Source LLC
LaVergne TN
LVHW021418110826
845150LV00007B/1983

* 9 7 8 1 4 2 5 5 0 9 4 5 3 *